THE PYRAMIDS

Greenwood Guides to
Historic Events of the Ancient World

The Peloponnesian War
Lawrence Tritle

The Reign of Cleopatra
Stanley Burstein

The Decline and Fall of the Roman Empire
James W. Ermatinger

The Trojan War
Carol G. Thomas and Craig Conant

The Emperor Justinian and the Byzantine Empire
James Allan Evans

The Establishment of the Han Empire and Imperial China
Grant Hardy and Anne Behnke Kinney

The Emergence of Buddhism
Jacob N. Kinnard

The Development of Ancient Technology
John W. Humphrey

The Emergence of Judaism
Christine Elizabeth Hayes

THE PYRAMIDS

Jennifer Hellum

Greenwood Guides to Historic Events of the Ancient World
Bella Vivante, Series Editor

GREENWOOD PRESS
Westport, Connecticut • London

Library of Congress Cataloging-in-Publication Data

Hellum, Jennifer.
The pyramids / Jennifer Hellum.
     p. cm. — (Greenwood guides to historic events of the ancient world)
    Includes bibliographical references and index.
    ISBN-13: 978–0–313–32580–9 (alk. paper)
    1. Pyramids—Egypt.   2. Egypt—Civilization—To 332 B.C.   I. Title.
  DT63.H45   2007
  932–dc22   2007016146

British Library Cataloguing in Publication Data is available.

Library of Congress Catalog Card Number: 2007016146
ISBN-13: 978-0–313–32580–9

First published in 2007

Greenwood Press, 88 Post Road West, Westport, CT 06881
An imprint of Greenwood Publishing Group, Inc.
www.greenwood.com

Printed in the United States of America

The paper used in this book complies with the
Permanent Paper Standard issued by the National
Information Standards Organization (Z39.48–1984).

10 9 8 7 6 5 4 3 2 1

CONTENTS

Series Foreword *by Bella Vivante*   vii

Preface   xiii

Timeline of Early Egyptian Dynasties and Kings   xv

Chapter 1   Historical Overview   1

Chapter 2   Egyptian Religion   17

Chapter 3   Symbolism of the Pyramids   35

Chapter 4   The Where and How of Pyramid Building   45

Chapter 5   The Pyramid Builders   55

Chapter 6   The Architecture and Art of the Pyramid Complex   67

Chapter 7   Interpretation and Legacy   81

Pyramid Profiles   89

Primary Documents   109

Glossary   129

Annotated Bibliography   135

Index   143

Photo essay follows Chapter 6

SERIES FOREWORD

As a professor and scholar of the ancient Greek world, I am often asked by students and scholars of other disciplines, why study antiquity? What possible relevance could human events from two, three, or more thousand years ago have to our lives today? This questioning of the continued validity of our historical past may be the offshoot of the forces shaping the history of the American people. Proud of forging a new nation out of immigrants wrenched willingly or not from their home soils, Americans have experienced a liberating headiness of separation from traditional historical demands on their social and cultural identity. The result has been a skepticism about the very validity of that historical past. Some of that skepticism is healthy and serves constructive purposes of scholarly inquiry. Questions of how, by whom, and in whose interest "history" is written are valid questions pursued by contemporary historians striving to uncover the multiple forces shaping any historical event and the multi-layered social consequences that result. But the current academic focus on "presentism"—the concern with only recent events and a deliberate ignoring of premodern eras—betrays an extreme distortion of legitimate intellectual inquiry. This stress on the present seems to have deepened in the early years of the twenty-first century. The cybertechnological explosions of the preceding decades seem to have propelled us into a new cultural age requiring new rules that make the past appear all the more obsolete.

So again I ask, why study ancient cultures? In the past year, after it ousted that nation's heinous regime, the United States' occupation of Iraq has kept that nation in the forefront of the news. The land base of Iraq is ancient Mesopotamia, "the land between the rivers" of the Tigris and

Euphrates, two of the four rivers in the biblical Garden of Eden (Gen. 2). Called the cradle of civilization, this area witnessed the early development of a centrally organized, hierarchical social system that utilized the new technology of writing to administer an increasingly complex state.

Is there a connection between the ancient events, literature, and art coming out of this land and contemporary events? Michael Wood, in his educational video *Iraq: The Cradle of Civilization*, produced shortly after the 1991 Gulf War, thinks so and makes this connection explicit—between the people, their way of interacting with their environment, and even the cosmological stories they create to explain and define their world.

Study of the ancient world, like study of contemporary cultures other than one's own, has more than academic or exotic value. First, study of the past seeks meaning beyond solely acquiring factual knowledge. It strives to understand the human and social dynamics that underlie any historical event and what these underlying dynamics teach us about ourselves as human beings in interaction with one another. Study of the past also encourages deeper inquiry than what appears to some as the "quaint" observation that this region of current and recent conflict could have served as a biblical ideal or as a critical marker in the development of world civilizations. In fact, these apparently quaint dimensions can serve as the hook that piques our interest into examining the past and discovering what it may have to say to us today. Not an end in itself, the knowledge forms the bedrock for exploring deeper meanings.

Consider, for example, the following questions. What does it mean that three major world religions—Judaism, Christianity, and Islam—developed out of the ancient Mesopotamian worldview? In this view, the world, and hence its gods, were seen as being in perpetual conflict with one another and with the environment, and death was perceived as a matter of despair and desolation. What does it mean that Western forms of thinking derive from the particular intellectual revolution of archaic Greece that developed into what is called rational discourse, ultimately systematized by Aristotle in the fourth century B.C.E.? How does this thinking, now fundamental to Western discourse, shape how we see the world and ourselves, and how we interact with one another? And how does it affect our ability, or lack thereof, to communicate intelligibly with people with differently framed cultural perceptions? What, ultimately, do we gain from being aware of the origin and development of these fundamental features of our thinking and beliefs?

In short, knowing the past is essential for knowing ourselves in the present. Without an understanding of where we came from, and the journey we took to get where we are today, we cannot understand why we think or act the way we do. Nor, without an understanding of historical development, are we in a position to make the kinds of constructive changes necessary to advance as a society. Awareness of the past gives us the resources necessary to make comparisons between our contemporary world and past times. It is from those comparisons that we can assess both the advances we have made as human societies and those aspects that can still benefit from change. Hence, knowledge of the past is crucial for shaping our individual and social identities, providing us with the resources to make intelligent, aware, and informed decisions for the future.

All ancient societies, whether significant for the evolution of Western ideas and values, or whether they developed largely separate from the cultures that more directly influenced Western civilization, such as China, have important lessons to teach us. For fundamentally they all address questions that have faced every human individual and every human society that has existed. Because ancient civilizations erected great monuments of themselves in stone, writings, and the visual arts—all enduring material evidence—we can view how these ancient cultures dealt with many of the same questions we face today. And we learn the consequences of the actions taken by people in other societies and times that, ideally, should help us as we seek solutions to contemporary issues. Thus it was that President John F. Kennedy wrote of his reliance upon Thucydides' treatment of the devastating war between the ancient Greek city-states of Athens and Sparta (see the volume on the Peloponnesian War) in his study of exemplary figures, *Profiles in Courage*.

This series seeks to fulfill this goal both collectively and in the individual volumes. The individual volumes examine key events, trends, and developments in world history in ancient times that are central to the secondary school and lower-level undergraduate history curriculum and that form standard topics for student research. From a vast field of potential subjects, these selected topics emerged after consultations with scholars, educators, and librarians. Each book in the series can be described as a "library in a book." Each one presents a chronological timeline and an initial factual overview of its subject, three to five topical essays that examine the subject from diverse perspectives and for its various consequences, a concluding essay providing current perspectives on the event, biographies of key players, a selection of primary documents, illustrations, a glossary, and an index. The concept of the series is to provide ready-reference materials that include a quick, in-depth examination of the topic, and insightful guidelines for interpretive analysis, suitable for student research and designed to stimulate critical thinking. The authors are all scholars of the topic in their fields, selected both on the basis of their expertise and for their ability to bring their scholarly knowledge to a wider audience in an engaging and clear way. In these regards, this series follows the concept and format of the Greenwood Guides to Historic Events of the Twentieth Century, the Fifteenth to Nineteenth Centuries, and the Medieval World.

All the works in this series deal with historical developments in early ancient civilizations, almost invariably postdating the emergence of writing and of hierarchical dynastic social structures. Perhaps only incidentally do they deal with what historians call the Paleolithic ("Old Stone Age") periods, from about 25,000 B.C.E. onward, eras characterized by nomadic, hunting-gathering societies, or the Neolithic ("New Stone Age"), the period of the earliest development of agriculture and hence settled societies, one of the earliest dating to about 7000 B.C.E. at Çatal Höyük in south-central Turkey.

The earliest dates covered by the books in this series are the fourth to second millennia B.C.E. for the building of the pyramids in Egypt, and the examination of the Trojan War and the Bronze Age civilizations of the eastern Mediterranean. Most volumes deal with events in the first millennium B.C.E. to the early centuries of the first millennium C.E. Some treat the development of civilizations, such as the rise of the Han Empire in China, or the separate volumes on the rise and on the decline and fall of the Roman Empire. Some highlight major personalities and their empires, such as the volumes on Cleopatra VII of Ptolemaic Egypt or Justinian and the beginnings of the Byzantine Empire in eastern Greece and Constantinople (Istanbul). Three volumes examine the emergence in antiquity of religious movements that form major contemporary world systems of belief—Judaism, Buddhism, and Christianity. (Islam is being treated in the parallel Medieval World series.) And two volumes examine technological developments, one on the building of the Pyramids and one on other ancient technologies.

Each book examines the complexities of the forces shaping the development of its subject and the historical consequences. Thus, for example, the volume on the fifth-century B.C.E. Greek Peloponnesian War explores the historical causes of the war, the nature of the combatants' actions, and how these reflect the thinking of the period. A particular issue, which may seem strange to some or timely to others, is how a city like Athens, with its proto-democratic political organization and its outstanding achievements in architecture, sculpture, painting, drama, and philosophy, could engage in openly imperialist policies of land conquest and of vicious revenge against any who countered them. Rather than trying to gloss over the contradictions that emerge, these books conscientiously explore whatever tensions arise in the ancient material, both to portray more completely the ancient event and to highlight the fact that no historical occurrence is simply determined. Sometimes societies that we admire in some ways— such as the artistic achievements and democratic political experiments of ancient Athens—may prove deeply troublesome in other ways—such as what we see as their reprehensible conduct in war and brutal subjection of other Greek communities. Consequently, the reader is empowered to make informed, well-rounded judgments on the events and actions of the major players.

We offer this series as an invitation to explore the past in various ways. We anticipate that from its volumes the reader will gain a better appreciation of the historical events and forces that shaped the lives of our ancient forebears and that continue to shape our thinking, values, and actions today. However remote in time and culture these ancient civilizations may at times appear, ultimately they show us that the questions confronting human beings of any age are timeless and that the examples of the past can provide valuable insights into our understanding of the present and the future.

Bella Vivante
University of Arizona

PREFACE

The pyramids are usually the first things people identify with the civilization of ancient Egypt. They are visible from space; as you fly into Cairo, even at night, the Giza pyramids seem to loom in the aircraft's windows. The size of the pyramids is of constant amazement to visitors. They are larger and more solid, in some way, than is imaginable. There simply don't seem to be enough superlatives to encompass their size. It is also little wonder that it seems an impossibility for humans to have built them, although the evidence is plentiful in humans' favor. It is wonderment, not mystery, that is their attraction, and understanding how they were built, how the manpower was organized, how the blocks were cut, what was important for the kings to include in the art in their mortuary and valley temples have all contributed to a feeling of wonder at the ingenuity and capability of humans.

The length of the Egyptian civilization as a whole is mind-boggling—almost exactly 3000 years. When one considers what was accomplished in the twentieth century alone, which opened with horse-drawn buggies, continued with walking on the moon, and closed with video-conferencing, in comparison the Egyptians seemed to have stagnated, a view far from the truth. Egypt did indeed look to their ancestors to help them make sense of the world, but they were well aware of the world outside their boundaries, and they undertook expeditions and began trading relations with the other countries of the ancient Near East from before the First Dynasty. As one of the earliest civilizations in that part of the world, and indeed, in any part of the world, the Egyptians watched others come and go, while maintaining their position of power. Part of that power lay in the mere presence of the pyramids—they have been tourist attractions almost from the moment they were built. It was considered to be a necessary portion of the rule of each king to visit the pyramids, to remember with wonder and respect the triumphs of their forefathers, and to leave graffiti that indicated they were there.

Perhaps one of the greatest differences between ancient Egypt and modern North America is the religion and the part it played in the society. Ancient Egyptian society was a religious society. Everything that happened in that society had a religious underpinning, from the festivals to the kingship to the agriculture to accounts and accounting. It is doubtful that it would have occurred to anyone to question the existence of the gods, although perhaps some were not as pious as others. It was that belief in a world that was governed by the gods and their actions that allowed for a situation in which the pyramids could be built. They were built for religious purposes, to announce the presence of the king to the gods in the afterlife, and as a result, they stand as testimonies to the strength of the Egyptian faith.

This book's first chapter sets the historical context for the building of the pyramids. Subsequent chapters focus on various aspects connected to the building of the pyramids, beginning with their place in early Egypt's religion and symbolic world view, the foundation for any understanding of ancient Egyptian culture. The chapters then continue to examine where and how the pyramids were built, the art and texts that covered walls, and the meaning these ancient wonders of the world continue to hold for humanity today. Due to the paucity of personal information, the Pyramid Profiles section profiles individual pyramids rather than people. Also included are a glossary of words not commonly used outside of Egyptology, and a series of original documents that tie in with various aspects of Egypt during the Old Kingdom, and in particular, tie in with pyramid building. It is intended that these will provide further dimensions to the book's primary contents.

Timeline of Early Egyptian Dynasties and Kings

All dates are approximate. Due to the difficulty of accurate dating in the earlier periods, particular dates cannot be assigned to the kings of the First and Second Dynasties.

All dates are B.C.E., "Before the Common Era."

3000   Egypt united as a country

3000–2686 EARLY DYNASTIC PERIOD

3000–2890 DYNASTY ONE:

Narmer

Aha—the earliest funerary enclosure discovered at Abydos, the first indication of the later pyramid complexes

Djer

Djet

Den

Merneith (queen)

Anedjib—evidence of mounds of mudbrick placed over the burial chamber of one of the king's courtiers, at Saqqara

Semerkhet

Qa'a

2890–2686 DYNASTY TWO: change of location for royal burials from Abydos to Saqqara

Hetepsekhemwy

Raneb

Nynetjer

Weneg

Sened

Peribsen—return to Abydos and building of funerary enclosure with tomb at Umm el-Qaab

Khasekhemwy—building of funerary enclosure at Abydos with tomb at Umm el-Qaab

2686–2160 THE OLD KINGDOM

2686–2613 DYNASTY THREE:

2686–2667 Nebka

2667–2648 Djoser—first to build a tomb in the shape of a pyramid, the Step Pyramid, at Saqqara, and the first to bring the enclosure and tomb together.

Imhotep—the famous architect of Djoser's pyramid

2648–2640 Sekhemkhet

2640–2637 Khaba

2637–2613 Huni—eleven small-step pyramids built up and down the Nile are attributed to Huni's reign

2613–2494 DYNASTY FOUR: the true Pyramid Age when the largest and most well-made of the pyramids were erected

2613–2589 Sneferu—first pyramid at Meidum and second, the Bent Pyramid, at Dahshur, both approx. 13 miles south of Giza; third, the Red Pyramid, the first true smooth-sided pyramid, about a mile north of Dahshur

2589–2566 Khufu—builder of the Great Pyramid at Giza

2566–2558 Djedefre (also known as Radjedef)—an unfinished pyramid at Abu Roash 5 miles north of the Giza Plateau, nearly straight across from the ancient sun-worshipping town, Heliopolis

2558–2532 Khafre—builder of the middle pyramid at Giza; at 471 feet it is 10 feet shorter than Khufu's next door, though it looks substantially larger

2532–2503 Menkaure—builder of the smallest pyramid on the Giza plateau

2494–2345 DYNASTY FIVE:

2494–2487 Userkaf—moves the royal burial ground from Giza to Abusir, about 7 miles south of the plateau

2487–2475 Sahure

2475–2455 Neferirkare

2455–2448 Shepseskare

2448–2445 Raneferef

2445–2421 Niuserre

2421–2414 Menkauhor

2414–2375 Djedkare

2375–2345 Unas—first king to use Pyramid Texts on the walls of the pyramid's chambers and entranceway; beginning of use of Saqqara (about 9 miles south of Giza) for royal burials, which continued into Dynasty Six

2345–2181 DYNASTY SIX: end of the Old Kingdom; widespread use of the Pyramid Texts by all the kings of the dynasty

2345–2323 Teti

2323–2321 Userkare

2321–2287 Pepi I

2287–2278 Merenre

2267–2184 Pepi II—included Pyramid Texts in the pyramid chambers of three of his queens, Neith, Iput II, and Wedjebten

2184–2160 Nitokris (queen)

CHAPTER 1

HISTORICAL OVERVIEW

THE PREDYNASTIC AND EARLY DYNASTIC PERIODS

The pyramids were built during one of the earliest periods in ancient Egyptian history, so early, in fact, that when Tutankhamun in the Eighteenth Dynasty recorded visiting them, they were already over a thousand years old. The societal processes that led to their construction, however, began much earlier. Generally, the history of the state and culture of ancient Egypt begins in the Archaic Period, in approximately 4000 B.C.E. The end of its history is somewhat arbitrary and subjective; it might be said to end with the Hellenistic Period (ca. 332 B.C.E.–395 C.E.), a time during which Egypt was ruled by Greece and, later, Rome. It was from the Hellenistic period that the culture of Egypt became an amalgam of Egyptian, Greek, and Roman cultures, never to regain its former stature as an individual state. The pyramids of Egypt, easily the most recognizable monuments of ancient Egypt, and perhaps of the ancient world, were built during the Old Kingdom (ca. 2649–2150 B.C.E.). This period followed the two earliest in Egypt's history, the Predynastic and the Early Dynastic Periods. The Predynastic Period includes the emergence of early cultures, the development of the Naqada culture, and Dynasty Zero (ca. 4000–2960 B.C.E.); the Early Dynastic Period includes Dynasties One and Two (ca. 2960–2649 B.C.E.); the Old Kingdom, Dynasties Three through Six. This chapter presents an overview of the political, societal, and governmental processes that were significant for understanding the importance the pyramids had for the people of Egypt, and more specifically, for the king.

Our knowledge of the succession of kings and certain events during their reigns comes from several native sources. The Palermo Stone, a list of kings up to the end of the Fifth Dynasty, is the earliest and only records the first five dynasties, plus a number of mythological dynasties prior to Dynasty One. The Turin Canon, a Ramesside papyrus with a fuller list of kings, dating from the thirteenth century B.C.E., is more complete and somewhat more reliable, although several of its assertions are contradicted by the archaeological record. It records the period from the beginning of Dynasty One to the Second Intermediate Period, between the Middle and New Kingdoms. Much later, in the third century B.C.E., a Greek priest named Manetho, living in the Delta town of Sebennytos, documented all the kings of ancient Egypt, using ancient texts. All of these sources are fragmentary; Manetho's comes down to us only through the work of other Greek authors, and both the Palermo Stone and the Turin Canon survive partially and only in pieces. With contemporary sources and corroboration from artifacts of the rulers themselves, however, it has been possible to put together a near-complete list of the rulers of ancient Egypt from the beginning of its history to the end.

The fundamental event in Egypt's history, the action that defined its character, and to some extent still defines the modern country, was the unification of the Two Lands; the Delta in the north, known as Lower Egypt, and the lands in the south, known as Upper Egypt. For the Egyptians, it was such a powerful symbol of the kingship and the character of the country that throughout the history of ancient Egypt, the rulers were known as the Kings of Upper and Lower Egypt. In practice, however, despite the dual crown the king wore indicating his rulership of Upper and Lower Egypt, the country was ruled as two major areas within one governmental state, and, with a few exceptions, not as two separate units. At some point around 3000 B.C.E., one Predynastic culture in Upper Egypt, the Naqada, a culture centered near the modern-day town of Naqada from which it takes its name, became the sole ruling polity in ancient Egypt. Whether this occurred as the result of one decisive battle, a series of hostile encounters, or as a peaceful subsuming of a number of smaller cultures in the north by this more dominant culture from the south is unknown and still hotly debated.

The Archaic Period ends with the unification of Egypt, and the Early Dynastic Period traditionally begins with the first period of dynastic rule, Dynasty One. There is substantial evidence, however, that the state of

Egypt was in place and functioning during the final stages of the Naqada period into Dynasty Zero, by approximately 3000 B.C.E. Ivory labels and sealings that identified the contents of pottery jars, inscriptions on other jars that identified the king and the royal estate of origin, imported Syro-Palestinian pottery—all these indicate the presence of a state administration firmly in place. Bureaucratic systems had to have been operating efficiently to manage foreign trade and royal landholdings of evidently substantial size, and the bureaucratic systems could not have run at all without a literate civil service. The idea of writing was assumed to have been borrowed from Mesopotamia where the earliest evidence of writing is found and certain styles of architecture and symbols in very early tomb reliefs clearly have their origins in Mesopotamia, rather than in Egypt. The styles of writing, both in terms of grammar and script, in Mesopotamia and in Egypt are so dissimilar, however, that they appear to have developed separately. By the Early Dynastic Period, writing had become an integral part of the Egyptian administration, a feature that allowed the bureaucracy to become more complex. Record keeping was fundamental to the running of the bureaucracy; it was integral to the documentation of the origin and location of both produce and manpower, and it was this documentation that made the building of the pyramids and their monumental architecture antecedents possible.

FIRST TO THIRD DYNASTY KINGS

While knowledge of the reigns of each king during the Early Dynastic Period is far from complete, particularly in detail, it is possible to put together broad impressions of certain reigns, such as those of Narmer and Den, and hence, understand, in sweeping terms, the beginnings of Egyptian history. There is some debate about the identity of the first king of Egypt, the debate generally being between Narmer and Aha. Keeping this controversy in mind, it will be assumed here that Narmer was the first king of the First Dynasty of ancient Egypt (ca. 3000 B.C.E.). His tomb at Umm el-Qaab, in Middle Egypt, the burial ground of the First and Second Dynasty kings beside Abydos, was discovered and excavated in the late nineteenth century. Other evidence for his reign includes ostraca or potsherds, pieces of broken pottery, inscribed with his name that were found at three separate sites in the northern Negev desert in Israel, as well as throughout the Delta and Upper Egypt. His name, written in a *serekh*, a rectangular enclosure meant to suggest the walls of the royal palace, has been found inscribed on the sides of a wadi, a dry riverbed, between the Nile Valley and the Red Sea. The geographical distribution of these artifacts attests to an early Egyptian presence in outlying areas, particularly in Syria-Palestine and in the eastern and western deserts on either side of the Nile Valley, and reinforces the notion that the Egyptian rulers were economically active throughout the region from the earliest periods of its history. This geographic reach did not end with Narmer, but continued through the rest of the Early Dynastic Period.

In terms of achievement, the reign of the fourth First Dynasty king, Den, is perhaps the most important after Narmer. Artifactual evidence for his reign shows considerable advancement in a number of different areas. A major progression in the architecture of tomb building, the use of a staircase to access the king's burial chamber, was introduced during this reign. This greatly eased the provisioning of the tomb, and was a measure that was adopted throughout Egypt in both royal and nonroyal tombs. The art of the reign is among some of the most beautiful and well-executed of the period, seen in the funerary goods of Hemaka, Den's chancellor and one of the most influential people in the country after the king. Included amongst the worked stone and wood objects, such as inlaid gaming discs, from this tomb is the oldest papyrus in Egypt, found in a circular wooden box. While the papyrus itself is anepigraphic, it indicates the use of papyrus at the earliest stages of Egyptian history. The art of this reign was viewed by following reigns in much the same positive way; objects inscribed with the name of Den have been found in the tombs of succeeding kings of the dynasty and elsewhere, included with the grave goods as heirlooms and items of value. The administrative advances, however, were the most important feature of this reign, having lasting impact on the rest of Egyptian history. It was during this reign that one of the most important titles of the king was introduced into the fivefold titulary, the five titles and attached names by which the king was known, the so-called *nsw-bity* (nesu-bity), the name of the king as ruler of Upper and Lower Egypt.

The Second Dynasty (ca. 2890–2649 B.C.E.) is largely unknown, due to a lack of archaeological evidence for events during the reigns of most of the kings of this dynasty, with the exception of the final two rulers, Peribsen and Khasekhemwy. Some time toward the beginning of the Second Dynasty, the capital of the country moved from Abydos in Upper Egypt to Memphis, at the apex of the Delta and the division between the

Two Lands. Following the reign of Ninetjer, the third king of the dynasty, there appears to have been a breakdown in the administration. The name of Ninetjer is not found outside the Memphis area, and this may indicate a restriction of the power and influence of the king at that time.

The two following kings, Weneg and Sened, are ephemeral, at best, with the reins of control not being decisively taken up again until Peribsen. For the first and last time, the *serekh* of Peribsen was surmounted by the Seth-animal, a mythological amalgam of a beast with a pointed snout, narrow pointed ears, and a tufted and bifurcated tail with a dog- or jackal-like body. Seth was the god of discord, trickery, and storms, the rival of Horus, his nephew, for the throne in the pantheon after the death of the divine King Osiris, who was Seth's brother and Horus' father. Horus was the god associated with the institution of kingship, and it is his figure, a falcon, that appears standing over the *serekh* of every king other than Peribsen and Khasekhemwy. It has been argued that the sudden appearance of Seth over the name of Peribsen is an indication that there was a rebellion by a rival faction, perhaps from a different part of the country, for the throne of Egypt at this time. Khasekhemwy's *serekh* is surmounted by both Seth and Horus, which might allude, in turn, to the reuniting of the two deities, and thus, the repelling of the intruding faction. The fact that one of the epithets found on seal impressions of Khasekhemwy, the succeeding king, is translated as "the Two Lands are at peace in him" has lent some credence to this argument, as the epithet might be an indication that the rebellion had been quelled by Khasekhemwy, bringing peace and unity once again to the Two Lands.

With the exception of the final two, the kings of the Second Dynasty chose to be buried at Saqqara, just south of Giza and modern-day Cairo. Possibly as a result of the use of Saqqara as a place of high-level burial, it became one of the five areas known collectively as the pyramid fields. The others are Giza primarily during the Fourth Dynasty, Abusir during the Fifth Dynasty, Dahshur during the early Fourth Dynasty, and Meidum during the Third Dynasty. The move represents a significant change from the previous dynasty's tradition, not only in place, but also in architecture. Previously, subsidiary graves of men and animals sent to their deaths to accompany the king into the afterlife, had been placed around the tombs and funerary structures of the kings, but with the advent of the Second Dynasty, subsidiary graves are no longer present.

The tombs of the First Dynasty were constructed with a tomb chamber surrounded by a series of storage rooms. Beginning in the Second Dynasty, the tombs were built as a series of galleries with storage rooms off a central causeway. This might have been a reflection of the end of the tradition of including subsidiary burials in the king's complex. Another significant change in the Second Dynasty funerary tradition is the apparent abandonment of the funerary enclosure of the First Dynasty. These were large areas enclosed by massive mudbrick walls, erected at Abydos close to the cultivation and approximately one mile from the tombs of the kings. They were used for funerary rites and cult rituals, and seem to have been torn down before the death of the next king. With the move to Saqqara, the kings of the Second Dynasty seem to have discontinued the practice of building the enclosures, and built only tombs. Primarily, this assumption is due to lack of hard evidence; it is possible that enclosures were built that haven't been found, but the evidence for this is conflicting. For the moment, it is best to assume that enclosures were not part of the Second Dynasty funerary ritual, until the two final kings, Peribsen and Khasekhemwy. They both had funerary enclosures at Abydos, heralding a brief return to the ancient royal necropolis.

The Third Dynasty (ca. 2649–2613 B.C.E.), like the Second, is largely unknown to us, with the dazzling exception of the reign of Djoser, also known as Netjerikhet, the first king of the dynasty. Despite the lack of information concerning the Third Dynasty, however, it is possible to give approximate lengths of reigns. It was under the rule of Djoser, which lasted for approximately 19 years, according to the Turin Canon, that the first pyramidally shaped major monumental superstructure was built. This is known as the Step Pyramid, and it is located in Saqqara. In terms of the administration of Egypt, however, the most significant development in the reign of Djoser was the institution of regular expeditions to the Sinai for the mining of turquoise, as opposed to the irregular and infrequent expeditions led during the previous dynasties. This was a sign of the advancement of the bureaucratic system that was now able to control the work done on behalf of the king at a fair distance outside of the traditional boundaries of the country.

EARLY DYNASTIC ADMINISTRATIVE ACHIEVEMENTS

The Early Dynastic and the beginning of the Old Kingdom Periods were a time of state formation, and the administrative achievements during this period were incorporated into Egyptian government until the demise of ancient Egypt. They seem to have been driven originally by the desire to control the trade routes with Palestine in the north and Nubia in the south. The goods traded along these routes were not everyday items, but rather, were prestige goods generally destined for use in the court. One of the methods for maintaining royal control is that of conspicuous consumption. Prominent use of foreign luxury trade goods indicates, at the very least, a presence in the geographical areas of trade, and to a subject populace, such an indication alludes to power. Examples of the type of items found that played a part in this process included silver from Anatolia in Turkey, obsidian from Anatolia, Arabia, and Eritrea, lapis lazuli from Afghanistan and Iran, turquoise from mines in the Sinai, and gold from Nubia, the latter two commodities often being collected by the Egyptians themselves.

A perhaps natural consequence of the impulse to control the trade routes from within Egypt was the desire to have power over the exportation of trade goods at the source. This became part of an expansionist program, evidence for which is seen in the presence of sealings, pottery, and typically Egyptian architecture in various sites around Palestine. If these finds can be interpreted as evidence for small Egyptian settlements within Palestinian town sites, then it seems inevitable that Egyptian administrative practices would have accompanied the settlers. Indeed, such relocation of governmental practices would have been necessary in order to maintain Egyptian control over these foreign sites, and thus, the administrative transplantation would have been deliberate. This is a practice seen in later imperial Egypt, during the Eighteenth Dynasty.

The economy was the impetus for the origins of writing, an indication of the powerful place the administration of the economy held in the governing of Egypt. The earliest records were ivory labels that were at one time attached to commodities such as jars of wine, recording the king under whose rule the produce was made, the amount of the produce, and the royal estate from which the produce came. Inherent in the process of labeling produce is the necessity for maintaining records of assets throughout the country. This entailed censuses of cattle, of men, and of "gold and fields," and required detailed records of the inundations of the Nile that were vital for the agricultural economy. The censuses were important for purposes of taxation, and royal landholdings throughout Egypt provided both places for the collection of taxes and major sources of revenue for the royal treasury.

It is significant that these landholdings reported directly to the capital, sending their products there for redistribution. The move of the capital from the south to the north was undoubtedly intended to create an administrative center on the borders of the two lands, and, indeed, it contributed substantially to the powerful and centralized government of the Old Kingdom. With the move to Memphis, however, the control of the south would have to have been tightly maintained, and it seems likely that royal visits to the south, in particular to Abydos, were regular, as a method of enforcing hegemony.

The hierarchy of the administration was of great importance during this period, and one's status within the hierarchy was often of greater consequence than the job one did while maintaining that status. The highest governmental officials in the Early Dynastic Period and the early Old Kingdom were members of the kings' families, and could be trusted as loyal servants. The position of "vizier," second in importance only to the king, first came into being during Djoser's reign. The men who held this position were the heads of the government and were solely responsible to the king for running every aspect of the administration. During the Third and early Fourth Dynasties, this position was held by princes of the royal family. Being the vizier allowed the holders of the title to accumulate great wealth to accompany the power, and the tombs of the viziers of this period show evidence of enormous wealth and power both in the architecture and the quality of the art adorning the tombs' walls.

Departments of the administration overseen by the vizier included the direction of mining expeditions to the desert, as well as the management of the desert mining areas. There were departments in charge of the *Sed* Festival, an ancient ritual also known as the Jubilee, and departments in charge of maintenance of the royal barges, indicating that royal travel during this period was significant. These areas of administration, mostly known to us via the lists of titles of the officials of this period, are undoubtedly but a small fraction of those actually comprising the total administrative organization.

One of the most important administrative innovations was the nomarchical system, likely instituted some time during the Second Dynasty. The two portions of Egypt were divided into nomes, which functioned like provinces or states. Eventually, there were twenty-two nomes in Upper Egypt and twenty-one in Lower Egypt, each one ruled by a nomarch. The status of the position of nomarch changed throughout Egypt's history, the nomarchy alternately being a royal appointment or an inherited situation. It is believed, although not conclusively, that the idea of a nomarchical system began in Lower Egypt. The earliest evidence for royal landholdings has been found in Lower Egypt, and it appears that the system of landholdings at the time was most extensive in this area. Royal landholdings, including royal estates and domains, provided the bulk of the royal treasury's possessions, and ensuring the continued revenue from these properties was very important to the economic well-being of the country. The nomarchs, as with the other high officials, were members of the royal family, and therefore, loyal and trusted. Later in the Old Kingdom, the nomarchy became an inherited position, and a contribution to the decentralization of the governmental administration.

THE FOURTH DYNASTY—MAJOR PYRAMID BUILDING

The Fourth Dynasty (ca. 2613–2494 B.C.E.) is the period during which the most famous pyramids, those on the Giza Plateau, were erected. By this time, the true pyramidal form of four steep and even sides leading to a peak became the rule, and the South Tomb turned into a mini-pyramid, a satellite structure. Sneferu (ca. 2613–2589 B.C.E.) was the first king to adopt the form we recognize today as a true pyramid. He is known to have built two pyramids at Dahshur, north of Meidum but south of Saqqara, and possibly two others, one at Meidum and a chamberless step pyramid at Seila, west of Meidum. The first of the Dahshur Pyramids is known today as the Bent Pyramid, due to a change in the angle of its incline approximately 162 feet from the desert floor. The ancient architects likely adjusted the angle in response to cracks that developed throughout the construction indicating that the original angle was too steep and unable to support the weight of the stone. The other pyramid at Dahshur, known as the Red Pyramid after a slightly pinkish cast to the stone in its core, lies a few kilometers north of the Bent Pyramid. It was taken as the tomb of Sneferu. The reasons for the necessity of building two separate pyramids are conjectural.

As a ruler, Sneferu was traditionally regarded as being kind and benevolent, while his son and successor, Khufu (or Cheops) was understood to be a tyrant. The only evidence for this is literary, and comes from three fantastical tales, two of which involve Sneferu and Khufu, written in the Middle Kingdom, approximately 500 years later (see Document 11). The first is a story in which Sneferu orders his court magician to retrieve a lost piece of jewelry that has fallen from a beautiful palace maiden to the bottom of the palace lake. In the second, Khufu demands that a learned man/magician cut the head off a prisoner and put it onto the body of another man. The magician objects to using the head of a human being and successfully suggests substituting the head of a cow. It is clear that some kind of tradition is being called upon in these stories that perceives of Sneferu as a kind and humble man, while Khufu is seen as someone who will arbitrarily kill a human being for the sport of seeing his head reattached to another body. Another factor that may have influenced later tradition regarding Sneferu is the meaning of his name, "The One Who Makes (Things) Beautiful;" however, Khufu's full name, Khnum-Khufu, can be translated as "May the God Khnum Protect Me," a statement neither demonstrably positive nor negative.

Whether this tradition held any truth is not known. Little remains of historical evidence for either king, beyond their pyramids and the state-sanctioned trade expeditions that were necessary to equip them. Most of the evidence for the trade expeditions lies in graffiti and rock inscriptions from quarrying and mining sites citing the names of different Third and Fourth Dynasty kings. While on trips north and south, the workmen, and often their superiors, frequently inscribed their names and the regnal dates of the current king on the rocks surrounding the mines and quarries. These provide evidence of both the presence of Egyptians and the dates during which they were present. Khufu's name has been found in quarrying sites in the western desert around Nubia. The Palermo Stone records a seafaring expedition during the reign of Sneferu to an unnamed place for a huge quantity of wood.

Khufu, Sneferu's successor, reigned for 23 years (ca. 2589–2566 B.C.E.) and was the ruler responsible for building the largest stone structure in the world, the Great Pyramid on the Giza Plateau. Although the center pyramid on the Giza Plateau, belonging to Khufu's son, Khafre, looks larger to the naked eye, the eastern-most pyramid in the row, Khufu's, is the largest. The construction of this pyramid, with its attendant labor and materials, was such a vastly larger undertaking than any project attempted previously that it has overshadowed both earlier and later pyramids in the modern public eye, although the total volume of quarried stone for Sneferu's pyramids is much greater.

The next king, Djedefre (ca. 2566–2558 B.C.E.), a son of Khufu, abandoned Giza as a pyramid site, and built his tomb at Abu Roash, to the north of Giza, across the valley from Heliopolis. The pyramid is largely destroyed now, and as a result, it is impossible to tell how large a structure it was. It seems likely that it was abandoned before it was finished; Djedefre is credited with only an 8-year reign. The reason for the move to Abu Roash may lie in the adoption by Djedefre of a new royal title, Son of Re. Heliopolis was, at this time, the center of the sun cult and the worship of the sun, Re, and the religious axis of the country. Thus, it was one of the most important cities in the Old Kingdom. The addition of the title Son of Re to the royal titulary indicates an emphasis on the sun god, hence on his worship, and on the king's relationship to him. The assumption of both the new title and the move to a place more geographically aligned with the primary location of sun worship are perhaps not coincidental events. At any rate, from this ruler on, with a very few exceptions, the remaining rulers of the Fourth Dynasty all had the name "Re" as an element of their own names, and the Son of Re title remained a part of the titulary until the end of pharaonic rule.

Khafre (ca. 2558–2532 B.C.E.) followed Djedefre, with a much longer reign of 26 years. Khafre moved the site of his pyramid back to Giza, to the west of Khufu's. It looks substantially larger than Khufu's; however, since it is built on bedrock approximately thirty-five feet higher than Khufu's pyramid and at a slightly sharper angle of slope, these two features cause the optical illusion of greater mass. As with all pyramids, whether step or regular, it is surrounded by an enclosure wall, which encloses the pyramid as well as a mortuary temple, with a causeway leading down to a valley temple.

The last of the three major pyramids on the Giza Plateau was erected by Menkaure (ca. 2532–2503 B.C.E.), during his 18- to 26-year reign. This is by far the smallest of the kings' pyramids, with only about one-tenth the mass of Khufu's pyramid. There may have been a number of reasons for this. With the advent of the addition to the titulary, it is reasonable to conjecture that it accompanied an addition or change to the religion and the regard with which the sun cult was held. This may, in turn, have led to a shift in the royal perception regarding the construction of funerary monuments the size and bulk of Khufu's and Khafre's. It is possible that the royal treasury placed more emphasis on the sun cult, its temples and endowments, and that such a shift in emphasis is attested in the decreased size of Menkaure's pyramid. It is without question that the building of his predecessors' pyramids put an enormous strain on the royal treasury, and such a strain might have had a significant impact on the amount of resources available for Menkaure to use.

The next ruler, Shepseskaf (ca. 2503–2494 B.C.E.), was the final king of the Fourth Dynasty, and he reigned for 5 or 6 years, according to the Turin Canon. He is the only king of this dynasty who did not build a pyramid; rather, he abandoned both the pyramidal tomb shape and the site of Giza, and built a huge sarcophagus-shaped mastaba in South Saqqara, instead. A mastaba was a rectangular stone structure erected on top of a tomb. They were often very large. As with so much else during this period, the reasons for the changes of shape and location are unknown. It is possible that these moves were the result of a change in religious ideology, and perhaps as well the result of a still further depleted treasury.

Other monumental constructions during this time were the provincial temples, erected during the reign of Menkaure. This was the beginning of the system of temple endowments from royal landholdings. Eventually, in the Eighteenth Dynasty and later, the landholdings became the property of the priesthoods, and the priests who were the beneficiaries of them became so powerful that the influence and wealth of the priests of these enormous temples and their endowments rivaled that of the king. In the Early Dynastic Period, however, the produce sent to the earliest temples came from landholdings still under royal control. The goods were used to feed and clothe the various levels of priest, and to present offerings to the deities to whom the individual temples were dedicated.

The building of the pyramids and provincial temples during the Fourth Dynasty required enormous amounts of manpower and finances, and the effect on the economy was profound. The men who worked to build the pyramids were not slaves; they were fed and housed as workers for the state, and recent excavations on the Giza Plateau have uncovered what may be a vast workman's village. It appears the state was responsible for feeding, clothing, and sheltering the workers during the periods of pyramid building. At one time, it was thought that the erection of such large-scale monuments occurred during the periods of seasonal inundation of the Nile. It seems, however, that the pyramids were more likely to have been built during the coolest months of the year; the inundation months were the hottest of the year, and unsuitable for such physical, heavy labor. It appears that the state did not skimp on the requirements for the workmen. To provide for this workforce, however, there needed to be an efficient system of taxation in place, particularly in terms of collection, as well as a centralized system of government. Both of these requirements were well in place during the Old Kingdom. The king was absolute ruler and, in theory, was also the owner of everything in the country. He was able to initiate such enormous work projects as the pyramids, as well as to ensure their completion.

THE FIFTH TO SIXTH DYNASTIES—END OF THE OLD KINGDOM

The Fifth Dynasty (ca. 2494–2345 B.C.E.) was a period of great religious change, in which the focus was firmly shifted from an emphasis on enormous funerary monuments to monuments dedicated to the worship of the sun. Pyramids continued to be built, but they were built of inferior materials and with construction techniques that proved to be inadequate for the longevity of the building. Of the nine rulers in this dynasty, the names of only three—Userkaf (ca. 2494–2487 B.C.E.), Menkauhor (ca. 2421–2414 B.C.E.), and Unas (ca. 2375–2345 B.C.E.)—were without the element of "Re." Until the reign of Unas, the site of Abusir, north of Saqqara by about 40 miles, now became the royal necropolis, with both pyramids and sun temples being built there. It is generally understood that this accompanied an ascendancy of the worship of the sun. With the elevation of Unas to the throne in about 2375 B.C.E., however, Abusir was abruptly abandoned and Saqqara once again became the royal necropolis. Whether this was the result of a new family coming to the throne, Unas being the first, or a desire on the part of Unas to have the necropolis closer to the capital at Memphis, or perhaps the signal of another change in the religion is unknown.

Perhaps linked to the necropolis shift from Abusir to Saqqara, is the appearance of funerary texts written on the walls of Unas' pyramid, and those of the Sixth Dynasty, that were intended to aid in the king's ascent to the skies and the company of the gods. These texts are known as the Pyramid Texts, and they constitute the earliest body of religious literature in the world (see Documents 12–17). They also constitute the first aspect of another portion of Egyptian history: prior to Unas, the various chambers of the pyramids had been without decoration of any kind, that being left to the walls of the mortuary temples, the causeways, and the valley temples within the pyramid complexes. Rather than a substitution, the Pyramid Texts were an addition to the reliefs in the pyramids' complexes, and were meant to be for the use of the deceased king. The texts also indicate a change in the practice of the religion; the kings were now given permanent aid in their heavenly ascension, and this shows a shift in the perception of both the kings' ascent and the role played by funerary texts.

A significant change occurred during the Fifth Dynasty that would affect the rest of the Old Kingdom, and might arguably have led to the passing of this period of innovation and advancement. This was the gradual disappearance of members of the royal family from the highest official positions in the bureaucracy of government, and in their place, the introduction of nonroyal functionaries. Generally, throughout the Fifth Dynasty, a trend toward individual effort resulting in individual reward increases, evidenced by the beautifully decorated and large mastabas of private individuals. This indicates that dependency on royal favor was at more and more of a remove, and that it was remotely possible to achieve an elevated social status through one's own efforts.

There was a gradual administrative shift during the later Old Kingdom of Dynasties Five and Six, partially seen in the switch from members of the royal family to wealthy commoners in positions of power, to the provinces from Memphis. The provincial centers began to flourish during this period, and the seat of government in the south changed several times, from Abydos to Thebes, with a number of other towns rising in importance, such as Coptos, just north of Thebes. Eventually, the location of Upper Egyptian government settled in Thebes, which remained one of the most important cities in southern Egypt for the next millennia.

Despite the internal changes at work, an Egyptian presence is still very much in evidence throughout the ancient Near East. Inscriptions from the Old Kingdom mention the procuring of timber for building from Byblos, on the Mediterranean coast, in modern-day Syria, and record the first mention of an expedition for incense to Punt. The exact location of Punt is still debated but it seems to have been on the eastern coast in the area of Eritrea and Ethiopia. Egyptian objects have been found at Ebla, also in modern-day Syria and other locations throughout the eastern ancient Mediterranean. While Egypt at this time did not have to worry about attacks from foreigners, and thus the period was a relatively peaceful one without major wars being fought, they still launched punitive actions against Libyan nomads to the west and Nubians to the south, as well as maintaining garrisons in the Sinai to protect the mining expeditions from Bedouin nomads. Pepi I of the Sixth Dynasty initiated several campaigns against Palestine, likely to keep the trade routes safe. Other trade routes, through the line of oases in the western desert to Aswan and Elephantine in the far south, were likewise guarded. At the entrance to Egypt south of Elephantine, as early as Sneferu, sturdy mudbrick fortresses at the first two cataracts were built to withstand sieges and traffic in and out of Egypt was carefully recorded and monitored.

There is literary and artistic evidence that at the end of the Fifth Dynasty and throughout the Sixth (ca. 2345–2181 B.C.E.), Egypt suffered from a drought, or perhaps a series of droughts. What little remains of the reliefs from Unas' causeway depicts seated men who are emaciated and clearly starving, with ribs showing and stick-thin arms hanging slackly by their sides, as if they hadn't the energy to lift them. The literary evidence for some kind of a natural disaster of this sort is from the Middle Kingdom, the period of time following the Old Kingdom and the First Intermediate Period. Various ancient authors speak of the results of natural disasters, including drought, and the accompanying disintegration of society. While it is not certain that the Old Kingdom is the period being discussed in these works, it seems likely that these events occurred toward the end of the Old Kingdom with the subsequent deprivation being felt in the succeeding period until the Middle Kingdom.

Pepi II (ca. 2278–2181 B.C.E.) was the last king of both the Sixth Dynasty and Old Kingdom. He has traditionally been credited with the longest reign of any ruler on earth, 94 years. Manetho states that he came to the throne as a child of six and ruled until his one-hundredth year. This huge, almost unbelievable span of time has been challenged over the years, and based on literary evidence, some Egyptologists feel that 70 years, still a very long reign, is a more reasonable length than 94. It is likely that, toward the end of his long life, the king gradually relinquished some, if not all, control of both his court and the provinces. Such a slow dispossession, coupled with a period of drought, would inevitably have advanced the decline of the period and led to the loss of governmental control during the First Intermediate Period. With the advent of this period, the dynastic rules significant for the building of the major pyramids in ancient Egypt came to an end.

CHAPTER 2

EGYPTIAN RELIGION

THE NATURE OF EGYPTIAN RELIGION

The religion of the ancient Egyptians was complex with different facets, tangents, methods of practice, and perceptions of the world surrounding them that provide some challenges to a modern understanding. Evidence points to the presence of a firm faith in a higher power, or, in this case, higher powers, a group of gods known as a pantheon. This faith was enacted in temples with rituals performed and festivals presided over by priests and, in the Old Kingdom, priestesses. The king was believed to be a divine being (see Documents 12 and 16). He was a god in his own right, to be worshipped as a god might be worshipped in a temple. This was a principle that had a very real impact on the society as a whole, and was directly responsible for the building of the pyramids.

After death, the Egyptians aspired to an afterlife, which, for the commoners, was identical to their life on earth. For the king, the afterlife was to be spent in the company of the gods, who were part of his family tree. This system of beliefs is quite different from those of modern religions. In other ways, however, the presence of a faith in the understanding of a greater-than-human force in the world is shared with most religions. The Egyptian faith, then, can be understood to be a religion, and not simply an aggregation of folk beliefs with only a tenuous dominant principle, as some historians have suggested.

Modern Western society is secular, for the most part, with a strict division between church and state. Ancient Egyptian society was nonsecular, which is to say it was permeated on every level with what we might today call "spirituality," and a religious/secular division of government and daily life would have been absolutely incomprehensible. The Egyptians lived with their religion as an intrinsic part of their existence, the reason for everything that surrounded them, the explanation for natural occurrences and man-made institutions. At the same time, the Egyptians were almost above all else an intensely practical people. When the religious ideas that lead to the construction of the pyramids are examined (below), it is clear that political pragmatism was as much a part of the reason for the creation of the pyramid complexes as religion.

The basic tenets and ideology of the religion of ancient Egypt were apparently set very close to the beginning of their history. From as early as the Second Dynasty, specific mention of gods in reliefs in commoners' tombs and votive offerings left to certain gods at places of worship have been found. Statuary evidence from the Archaic Period of an organized worship of the fertility god, Min, has also been discovered. The late Fifth Dynasty Pyramid Texts, the earliest works of Egyptian religious literature, provide evidence of the existence of a well-developed pantheon and ideology already in place in the twenty-fourth century B.C.E. What is truly remarkable about this is the fact that the ideology evident in the earliest texts and artifacts remained the underlying ideology for the rest of ancient pharaonic Egyptian history. Certain changes were instituted in different parts of the history, but these did not affect the fact of the worship of deities and the understanding of an afterlife to which every Egyptian might aspire. Hence, the texts, art, and artifacts point to the conclusion that a common religious faith, based on shared beliefs, was a part of Egyptian culture from the earliest periods of the history.

A common modern perception of ancient Egyptian religion is one of a faith obsessed with death. This is the result of the disproportionate amount of archaeological evidence that is funerary in nature, and is a perception that is being laid to rest, in recent years, with the excavation of town sites, in which religious artifacts play a more peripheral part. In fact, the wonderful reliefs found in the tombs of the wealthier Egyptians reveal a great deal about daily life on earth. These pictorial representations of ordinary Egyptians at work and at leisure help immeasurably to put nonfunerary artifacts in the context of everyday, normal events in the lives of ancient Egyptians. It is possible to extrapolate from these reliefs an ancient emphasis on life continuing as it had in earthly existence, which, in turn, leads to the conclusion that life was an ideal and treasured state.

EGYPTIAN DEITIES

The fundamental doctrine of Egyptian religion lay in polytheism, which is the worship of a multitude of deities. In Egypt, the pantheon had well over two hundred different lesser and greater deities. The king himself was considered to be of divine birth, a notion that was reinforced by the royal office, which was itself embodied in Horus, the falcon god of the kingship. The gods were worshipped as entities that were present on earth and in the *duat*, the Egyptian afterworld, and they were able to move between the two realities with ease. While on earth, they resided in their cult statues deep within the temple proper in a room called "the holy of holies," seen only by the lector priest, or *heri-heb*. While in the sky and the *duat*, they lived in a world that seems to have been different things at different times. The Pyramid Texts describe the world of the gods as one similar to earth, with a river running through it upon which the sun, Re, sailed in a boat during the day. The boat of the sun was crewed by the ancestors of the king and by the most important of the gods. It was this company that the king aspired to join after death.

Temples were erected in many cities throughout ancient Egypt. Each temple was dedicated to the worship of one main deity, but often included chapels for the worship of other deities within the temple walls. Shrines have been found in commoners' houses in excavations of town sites, particularly Tell el-Amarna, an Eighteenth Dynasty city that was abandoned soon after the death of the king, and Deir el-Medina, the town of the artisans who sculpted and painted the royal tombs in the Valleys of the Kings and Queens during the New Kingdom. The shrines were generally dedicated to deities deemed to have an immediate impact on the lives of ordinary Egyptians. This included gods such as Bes and Hathor. Bes was a dwarf figure with a frightening face. His tongue was always stuck out but he was actually quite a joyous deity, and was the protective god for women in labor. Hathor was a cow goddess and the goddess of happiness and music, a goddess worshipped especially by women. Her counterpart, Sekhmet, was a terrifying lion goddess who, in one myth, attempted to destroy mankind for Re by devouring them. Judging from this evidence, it appears that the deities and supplication to them were not only in the sphere of the king, but were part of the daily lives of every Egyptian, regardless of social standing.

Most of the deities had a number of spheres of influence under their purview. Thoth, for example, was the god of writing and scribes, and more abstractly, of intelligence and justice. He was generally shown as an ibis[bird]-headed male figure or as a baboon, demonstrating the very different significance this animal held for the ancient Egyptians. In scenes of the underworld, he was always placed in ibis-headed form, recording names, standing beside the scales on which the heart of the deceased was weighed against the feather of truth. He was also a moon-god, an attribute he shared with another lesser god, Khonsu. These features, scriptorial and lunar, were distinct and without apparent similarity, yet they were to be considered to coexist as part of the complex personality or character of Thoth. Overall, this intricacy of characteristics was true of all the deities with some appearing to be more fully developed than others, and a few growing in complexity through the years of worship. One deity who became more complicated was Isis, who grew from primarily supporting role in the Heliopolitan cosmogony, or creation myth, to become a deity worshipped throughout the ancient Mediterranean world by Hellenistic Greek and Roman times.

SYNCRETISM

A trait peculiar to Egyptian religion is syncretism, or amalgamating two or more deities to make one, without the original deities losing their place or character in the pantheon. Thus, three gods were created from two, or four were created from three. This was particularly evident during the New Kingdom; however, there is evidence of the process of syncretization from the Pyramid Texts. Perhaps the most important of the syncretized deities was Amun-Re, worshipped during the New Kingdom in particular. Amun-Re was a distinct and separate deity, while Amun and Re themselves retained their individual characters. Amun-Re was endowed with qualities from both Amun and Re, which gave him a character different from either of the individual deities. Primary among the differences in divine qualities is the intimate connection Amun-Re had with the office of kingship, represented as Horus. Amun and Re on their own were deities most closely involved with the natural world, while Amun-Re was a royal deity, almost becoming a divine alter-ego for the living king.

Horus and Amun-Re, the two most important deities that were associ-ated with the king, each had their own purview or specialization. Horus was the god of kingship, not the king. He was responsible for the office of the king, the ruling of Egypt, rather than the ruler of Egypt. Amun-Re, on the other hand, was a powerful syncretization of the two most im-portant deities in the pantheon, looking after the king himself, ensuring his well-being and strength. The combination of the two—Re, the "sun", and Amun, the "hidden one"—united both the seen and the unseen. The sun was the most significant natural factor in the lives of the Egyptians; as a naturally occurring object, it had complete power over their daily lives. Perhaps only the Nile and the deserts were as important, but it was to the sun that the dead king journeyed in the afterlife. Amun, as the "hidden one," was all the more powerful because he was invisible, hence omniscient. He held authority over the mysteries of life and death, and everything between, particularly religion. The melding of these two formidable deities into one created a deity with dominance over two of the most significant aspects of the lives of the ancient Egyptians, the natural and the unknown, unnatural worlds.

The Egyptians performed this kind of religious manipulation adeptly and with no uncertainty or awkwardness, and their acceptance of such apparent inconsistencies was likely one of the reasons for the longevity of their system of beliefs. It allowed for change and mutation both of form and of character, qualities that led to a certain amount of amorphousness of understanding, an ability to move with the religious wind. In allowing for such qualities, the religious thought remained supple and malleable, able to withstand three thousand years of religious accretion and accumu-lation. Incorporating new deities, even foreign deities, into the Egyptian pantheon required boundaries of faith that were able to accept differing interpretations of divinity and godhood. Having such pliant boundaries meant that the faith of the ancient Egyptians was neither dogmatic nor fossilized, two characteristics that allowed it to change and adapt to new ideas and interpretations.

PANTHEON

The pantheon has been explained as existing in "constellations" or amorphous groupings of deities. The groups tend to have three deities (a triad), eight deities (an ogdoad), or nine deities (an ennead). This is a convenient method of explaining the various relationships between them, and it has the advantage of presenting the deities outside of a hierarchy, something that is helpful in coming to terms with the various facets of divine purview. Thus, although Re, the god of the sun's energy and light, was worshipped throughout Egypt's history as the life-giver to the world, sun-worship was not in ascendancy, except during the Old Kingdom and in particular, the Fifth Dynasty. At other periods, other deities' priesthoods were wealthier, and hence, more powerful, a circumstance that did not lessen Re's place in the pantheon. As the life-giving sun, his place was of fundamental importance to the world as a whole, something that ensured his continued worship, whether on a grand or lesser scale. It was thus with most of the deities most often mentioned in religious texts and carved in relief on tomb walls. They existed as a congruity of parts, rather than as a hierarchical body. The type of worship or, perhaps better, the level of worship the deities received on earth was driven more by human political considerations than by the deities' positions in the pantheon. Whether this was held to be true by the ancient Egyptians themselves is something that modern scholars will never know as a certainty but it will surely be the focus of endless debate amongst them.

The "constellations" that had the greatest impact on Egyptian religion during the Old Kingdom were those connected to a cosmogony, or myth of the birth of the world, specific to the city of Heliopolis and through that, to the office of the kingship. The Egyptians had a number of different cosmogonies, each centered in different cities and each with a different first deity. The Heliopolitan cosmogony and the concerns of the deities involved are directly relevant to both the political and religious philosophies of the Old Kingdom. The cosmogony begins with the creation by Atum, the first god and emergence of a primeval mound from the watery abyss, the Nun (pronounced "Noon"). Standing upon this original piece of earth, Atum dispelled darkness by creating light, in the form of the sun, Re. Having begun the world, Atum then created air, the god Shu, and moisture, the goddess Tefnut ("Tef-noot") (see Document 15), who in turn together created earth, the god Geb, and sky, the goddess Nut ("Noot"). Geb and Nut brought into existence Osiris, the first king of Egypt and the eventual god of the underworld, Isis, his consort/sister, Seth, his brother/enemy, and Nephthys, wife of Seth and companion of Isis. The union of Osiris and Isis resulted in the falcon god of the Egyptian kingship, Horus. Once Atum had begun the process of the now self-propelled creation of the Heliopolitan Ennead, he changed into a *benu* bird, a type of heron, and flew to the top of the *benben* stone, a stout obelisk that was emblematic of the worship of the sun.

Of further importance to the religion implicit in the construction of the pyramids is the myth of the death of Osiris at the hands of his brother Seth (see Document 13). Osiris, having held the throne for many years, was murdered by his brother, Seth, the god of confusion and chaos, through trickery and deceit. Seth then had Osiris' body dismembered and the pieces thrown all over Egypt. Isis, with the help of Nephthys, both in the form of predatory birds known as kites, gathered the parts together, and from the reconstituted Osiris, Isis was impregnated with a son, Horus. After Osiris' reconstitution, he became the god of the afterlife, responsible for judging souls and often supplicated to by commoners in their tomb reliefs, while Horus, his son, took over the purview of the kingship.

THE KING'S PLACE IN EGYPTIAN BELIEF

The reigning king was a part of that purview; hence, he was part of the character of Horus, as well as being protected by the god. As the gods were seen as being harmonious parts of the whole, so was the king seen as a harmonious part of Horus and the essence of the god was in him, protecting him as the human ruler of Egypt. The divine king was of paramount consequence both within the religious faith of the Egyptians and for the sake of political expediency. Divine rulers were at the top of the social human hierarchy, and were unassailable, directly as a result of their divinity. On a less celestial level, rulers who were understood to be part of the supernatural world naturally wielded power that no-one else could match. It was this idea that allowed the Old Kingdom kings to command that a pyramid be built, and to have that command carried out. The idea itself was given a religious underpinning by the myth of Osiris' death. When the reigning king died, he left the collective nature of Horus and entered the collective nature of Osiris, while the new king took in the essence of Horus. The deceased king became known as the "Osiris So-and-so," for example, the Osiris Unas or the Osiris Pepi.

The afterlives of the king and his subjects seemed to follow their earthly duties and desires. The afterlife of the wealthy commoner, and generally that included everyone except the king and, in the late Old Kingdom, the queen, was a landscape identical to Egypt, evidence for which being found in the reliefwork of their tombs. The afterlife of the less-wealthy or poor Egyptians is a mystery, as they couldn't afford to have much more than holes in the ground as their final resting places, the bodies often only wrapped in linen without even a coffin. As a result, it is unknown whether they aspired to an afterlife at all, much less what that afterlife might have been like.

In ancient Egypt, which for the Egyptians meant the world, the king was the most important person, and as such, he was understood to be re-sponsible for the maintenance of the universe by symbolically performing each ritual in each temple throughout Egypt at the same time everyday. This was clearly impossible; thus, the highest levels of Egyptian priests from one end of Egypt to the other were understood to adopt the guise of the king, in order to perform, in his absence, those rites that it was vital he perform in each temple at the same time.

After death, the deceased king rose into an afterlife in the east, and the metaphor on earth for that rebirth was the reappearance of the sun each morning, having "died" the previous sunset in the west. The king was understood to join the sun-god, Re, in his barque on the daily journey through the sky. In order that he would remain part of the universe and, by his presence in the sun-barque, stabilize the world and prevent chaos from encroaching, the king was maintained in the afterlife with food, drink, and veneration in the mundane world. This was accomplished by performing rituals in the mortuary temples on a daily and nightly basis. The morning rites greeted the king and the sun together as one entity. The evening rites both bid them good bye and made their return a certainty. Regular implementation of the rites helped ensure that the king was given the necessary offerings to keep him alive in the afterlife, and able to preserve his position in the sun-barque, maintaining the equilibrium that kept the world together (see Documents 3, 4, 8, and 9). The temples were specifically situated on the east side to ensure that the diurnal and nocturnal mortuary rites would, on a symbolic level, become part of the royal funerary myth that involved the ascent of the king to his heavenly afterlife.

The king's presence in the sky was determined by the reliefs in his complex. A band or frieze of depictions of provisions around the tops of the walls of the sanctuary would have provided the same sustenance as the rites enacted on the king's behalf. These reliefs represented the vitality of each day in the king's life, in terms of living male and female servants bringing just-made or just-picked offerings or living creatures. While on earth, the king could expect such provisions to have been available everyday in abundance, brought into the undoubtedly busy palace for meal preparation by servants. Often, in the mortuary temple reliefs, the bearers were officials of the king, who gained immortality through their presence in the reliefs.

THE RELIGIOUS NATURE OF THE PYRAMID COMPLEXES

Each of the pyramid complexes comprised the pyramid, a mortuary temple, generally on the east side of the pyramid, an enclosure wall surrounding the pyramid and mortuary temple with a covered causeway leading down to the Nile bank, to a valley temple used for the arrival of the king's body by boat. The mortuary temple was the primary place for the enactment of ritual, which, in the case of this particular style of temple, was for the cult of the dead king. The cult was specifically intended to sustain the deceased king in the afterlife, providing his soul and spirit with food and worship. The walls of the mortuary temple, the causeway, and the valley temple were carved in relief and then painted. They generally depicted the king with various deities and, unlike the tombs of commoners, not the intimate scenes of daily life.

The first mortuary temples may well have been the small chapels within the Early Dynastic Enclosures at Abydos. These enclosures were the first royal architectural mortuary features in Egypt above ground and they were separated from the tombs of the corresponding kings by one and a half miles, the tombs being at Umm el-Qaab to the west against the cliffs of the high desert. The chapels and the enclosure walls were mudbrick, and consisted of two accessible rooms and one apparently inaccessible room. The floor plans are all that remain of the structures, but these are enough to indicate door thresholds to two rooms and no readily obvious entrance to the third. It is possible that this is the earliest evidence of the serdab, a statue room in the later pyramid complexes that was without a door but that almost always had a small opening through which the statues inside could magically see out and thus participate in the rituals being conducted in the other room or rooms. Some of the enclosures were paved with mud floors; it is likely that all the enclosures had them, but that being extremely fragile and difficult to excavate, they have been destroyed.

The presence of the cult buildings within the enclosures' walls in the absence of anything else is one of the two primary differences between the enclosures of the Early Dynastic Period and those of the Old Kingdom. The other difference is in the temporal role the enclosures played in the Early Dynastic kings' funerary cults. It appears the earlier structures were built as nonpermanent constructions, and were pulled down some years after their erection. Exactly when they were destroyed is unknown; it is possible that they were demolished in anticipation of the construction of a new wall for the successor to the throne, perhaps in time for his death. Careful archaeological excavation has shown, however, that the dismantling of the buildings was deliberate, and that the walls were made in such a way as to make the dismantling a relatively quick and easy procedure. This was accomplished by stacking bricks one on top of the other, without interlocking them to create stability. By piling the bricks several layers, hence meters, thick, the pressure of the bricks against one another created an inherent stability. The wall would have lost that stability once the process of demolition had begun, and the surrounding solidifying force removed.

It is believed that the need for the enclosure walls arose from the need for sequestered sacred space, for the performance of the cult rituals involved in worshipping the dead king. The reason for this need lay in the nature of the rituals, specifically the notion that rituals are enactments of myth, intended to re-create the divine circumstances and consequences of myth. Such re-creations are intended to bring the divine world into a selected space of the mundane, or everyday, world, and such a space needs to be protected from harm, as well as to protect those uninitiated who might conceivably be harmed by its divine power. The enclosure wall surrounding the pyramid and the mortuary temple performed exactly this function; it kept the rituals and enacted myths far from harm and away from those not invested with a priesthood and the requisite purity. Consequently, this type of space, and the artifacts used in the rituals performed in the space, often had to be deconsecrated when their ritual functions ended. This meant either the burial or destruction of statues and ritual implements, or the razing of religious buildings. Such seems to have been the case with the enclosure walls of the Early Dynastic Period; however, the cults of the deceased kings of the Old Kingdom often continued for long periods of time following the burial of the king, even into the reigns of several successors, and perhaps as a result, the walls surrounding the pyramids do not seem to have suffered the same deliberate demolition.

MORTUARY TEMPLES

The mortuary temples of true pyramids (as opposed to step pyramids such as Djoser's), with one exception, were located against the east side of the pyramid, generally, although not always, abutting the face of the pyramid itself. The only pyramid with a mortuary temple on a side of the pyramid other than the east side is that of Userkaf of the Fifth Dynasty. The mortuary temple of this pyramid's complex was built on the south side of the pyramid, as the east side abutted a steep rise in the ground, leaving no room for a full-sized building. The sanctuary was built on the eastern side, however, to place it in the path of the early morning sun's rays.

The architectural progression from the earliest temple at Meidum to the later temples at Giza was one going from the barest simplicity to a great deal more complexity. The temple at Meidum was merely two rooms, one an entrance hall and the other a sanctuary, where the business of ritual and prayer took place. The materials used in the construction of this and other Old Kingdom mortuary temples, until the erection of the great pyramids at Giza, are mudbrick and limestone of no particular quality, and the interior walls appear to be devoid of decoration. In fact, the only evidence that the walls might have been decorated is found in the remains of the Northern Pyramid of Sneferu at Dahshur, in which representations of the king performing certain rites at his *Sed* Festival have been found in sculpted relief.

Beginning with Khufu's complex, the mortuary temples have the following rooms: entrance hall, open cloistered court, five niches for statues of the king, magazines for storage of ritual tools and offerings, and sanctuary. Each of these fulfills an important purpose in the rituals carried out on behalf of the dead king. The growth in number from two for Sneferu's temple at Meidum to well over five for the temple of his son, Khufu at Giza indicates a broadening in both the rituals and the understanding of the role of the king in the religious affairs of Old Kingdom Egypt. The greater number of rooms indicates a growing importance and presence of the king in the afterlife, a feature that may have extended from a growth in importance during the king's rule on earth. The fact that this expansion of the royal role occurred quite suddenly from the reign of Sneferu to the reign of Khufu is perhaps a suggestion of the character of Khufu, who was regarded later in Egyptian history to have been a tyrant, a cruel ruler who worked his subjects to death and put many of them into slavery.

CAUSEWAYS AND VALLEY TEMPLES

The causeways and valley temples, also known as valley buildings, were integral parts of the pyramid complexes. Although they did not have the same cultic importance that the mortuary temples and enclosure walls did, they were vital in other ways. The causeways were walled-in corridors that led from the eastern walls of the enclosures to the valley temples; the earliest causeways seem to have been unroofed, while the later ones were roofed either with blocks of stone or, rarely, with logs. In order to admit light into the otherwise completely dark corridors, the builders used one of two methods of providing clerestory lighting; either they cut slits into the roofing slabs, or they positioned the slabs or logs so that they did not touch in the middle, leaving a narrow band of area open to the sky. For the most part, the causeway walls were made of limestone blocks, generally battered to some degree and rising from 6 feet to 13 feet. They ranged in width from 8 feet 8 inches (Unas) to 15 feet (Khafre), and in length from 235 yards (Meidum) to 750 yards (Unas). The inner walls of the later causeways were decorated with sculpted reliefwork, although Unas' is the only causeway with enough remaining to show a relatively complete program of decoration.

Until the pyramid of Unas, the last king of the Fifth Dynasty, the pyramids themselves were empty of decoration, which was only included in the temples that were part of the pyramid complexes, the mortuary temple and the valley temple. Unas' pyramid was the first one in which Pyramid Texts were inscribed, and the tradition continued past the Old Kingdom and ended with the ephemeral kings of the First Intermediate Period.

The enclosure wall and the covered causeway ensured that the entire complex was safe from the eyes of commoners and nonpriests. This was a very important consideration not only in the practice of the cult of the dead king, but in religious ritual and cult in general. For the most part, with the exception of public festivals, particularly in the New Kingdom, all religious rituals in the temples were performed in secret, a custom that was the result of "decorum,"[1] or the hierarchization of knowledge. Decorum is the notion that religious knowledge, and principally, knowledge attached to ritual and cult, was dispensed according to a hierarchy. The chief priests, of whom the king was the highest, were admitted to the ownership of all pertinent knowledge regarding the cultic practices, knowledge that amounted to everything that was needed to keep the world in spiritual order. The further down the hierarchical ladder one's priestly office stood, the less knowledge one was allowed to possess concerning daily and nightly temple activities. Whether this worked in practice or in theory only is debatable; however, it is certain that the common populace were forbidden access to the inner sancta of the temples and only saw the cult statues on festival days, which occurred with some frequency.

PRIMEVAL MOUND

The primeval mound is a symbolic association that can be found in Egyptian architecture as early as the First Dynasty. During the excavation of a mastaba in North Saqqara from the reign of Anedjib, the seventh king of the dynasty, it was discovered that the tomb chamber was covered with a stepped mound of clean, sterile sand, and above that, a mound of the same type of sand covered the entire tomb. All of this was encased in the mastaba superstructure, which meant that it was never intended to be seen. While this is the earliest unequivocal evidence for this type of construction, there seems to have been a similar structure within the tomb of the predecessor of Den, the fourth king of Dynasty One. The belief in an afterlife, together with the idea of a clean and sterile mound of sand representing the original birth of the world, gives the tombs' mounds a profound religious symbolism. The sand, as primeval mound, lent its generative and emblematic powers to the dead body over which it lay, helping create the circumstances in which the soul of the person might rise to live in the afterlife. The stepped construction of these interior mounds would seem to be the antecedent of the Third Dynasty Step Pyramid of Djoser, itself the antecedent of the true pyramids of the Fourth Dynasty and on. The superstructures of these larger monuments acted in the same religious manner as the interior structures of the smaller mastabas and tombs. This provided the Egyptians with a tangible connection to an intangible concept, creating a bond between the earthly world and the world of the afterlife, and lending each a few of the properties of the other.

It is likely that by the time the idea of the primeval mound as funerary monument reached its culmination in the pyramids, it had grown and matured, taking on other meanings and symbolism. Egyptian religious ideology could accept and incorporate a number of disparate ideas as a natural process, and thus, the other meanings and symbolisms were plausible, simultaneous with that of the pyramid as primeval mound. It is possible that the shape of the pyramid was influenced by the visible rays of the sun, which at times appear to stem from a point in the heavens and fan out as they descend to earth. Another possibility is a modified staircase to heaven, providing an elevated point from which the deceased king could finally ascend to the company of the gods.

WORSHIP OF RE

During the Old Kingdom, the sun was the primary feature of worship. This reached its apogee during the Fifth Dynasty. Of the nine kings recorded for this dynasty, all but three, Userkaf, Menkauhor, and Unas, had the element of Re as part of their name. Three kings of the Fourth Dynasty and one in the Sixth Dynasty also had names that included the sun-god, indicating, perhaps, that there was an increase in sun-worship during the Fourth Dynasty into the Fifth, with a relatively sudden drop in popularity in the Sixth. Theophoric names, particularly royal names, are often a reliable indicator of prevailing religious thought; for the Fifth Dynasty, there is architectural evidence, as well, in the form of sun temples, a particular style of temple found only during this period. With the exception of Djedkare-Isesi, the penultimate king of the dynasty, and Unas, each king of the Fifth Dynasty erected a sun temple and a pyramid at Abusir, south of Saqqara. There is literary evidence for each temple; however, only two of the sun temples have been found, those of Userkaf and Niuserre. All the pyramids, except Menkauhor's, have been discovered and excavated. Djedkare-Isesi chose to build only a pyramid at South Saqqara, rather than at Abusir, and Unas followed suit.

The sun temple complexes were very similar to the pyramid complexes, with a valley temple and a covered causeway leading to another temple in the higher desert. The focus of the upper temple precinct was a very large squat obelisk, the *benben* stone, standing on a platform that somewhat resembled the primeval mound in shape. In Niuserre's complex, a place for offerings was located in front of the obelisk. Four large alabaster representations of the hieroglyph meaning "to satisfy," a rectangle topped with a stylized conical loaf of bread, were laid on their sides and placed in a square, with a stone representation of the sun, which was also the hieroglyph for the name of Re, in the middle of the square. Pointing to the four cardinal directions, this read "May Re be satisfied." There are channels and runnels carved into the stone, perhaps with the intention that the blood of offerings of sacrificed animals would run off them. This was open to the sky, as befitted an altar dedicated to the sun, and within the enclosure walls, it was accompanied by various other features that seem to be places of sacrifice.

An archive of administrative papyri was found in the pyramid complex of Neferirkare that illuminates some of the activities of the priesthood attached to his sun temple. The records show rosters of the different phyles of the temple, the diurnal and nocturnal religious rituals they performed, and the types and quantities of offerings. They also reveal the day-to-day working of the temple, including the changeovers from phyle to phyle, documenting damage to temple furniture and levels of offerings in the storerooms. It becomes apparent, particularly in the papyri dealing with ritual and personnel, that the rituals of the sun cult were intended to maintain the universe. Nocturnal rituals involved keeping track of the stars from the roof of the temple, making the proper presentations of offerings at the proper time to ensure the return of the sun in the morning. Diurnal rituals were concerned with the various and many festivals that occurred celebrating the king and the pantheon. Commoners were understood to operate as servants of the gods, and the gods depended on them for food, drink, and supplication.

PRIESTLY AND WOMEN'S ROLES

There were several different priestly offices, including the *wab*-priest or "purity" priest, the *henti-shay* or palace attendant, the *hem-ka* or servant of the spirit, the *sem*-priest whose function is not completely understood, the *hem-netjer* or "god's servant," and the lector priest. Each was responsible for certain tasks in the day-to-day running of the temple, although evidence from the Abusir Papyri seems to indicate that the tasks were interchangeable, as perhaps were the offices themselves. The lowliest priestly office was the *wab*-priest, the highest the "god's servant" and the lector priest. In terms of the temple hierarchy, the lector priest was the only priest allowed into the inner sanctum, the "holy of holies" where the cult statues "lived." They were responsible for bringing offerings, "waking" the statues (in other words, bringing the spirit of the deity into its corporeal representation), and clothing them each day. They were also responsible for a wonderfully practical part of the cult, known as the "reversion of offerings." This ritual saw the offerings that were placed before the god's or king's cult statue removed by the lector priest for redistribution to the priests of the attendant phyle, and his footsteps swept away to leave an inviolate space for the privacy of the deity inhabiting the statue. As a result, the food offerings were not left to rot but were given to the priests as part of their stipend. The essence of the god within the cult statue had presumably consumed the essence of the offerings, leaving the earthly remains for those of the earth.

Women's Roles

The role of women in the religious life and rituals in the Old Kingdom was considerably greater than at any other period in Egypt's history. They performed in the roles of three different types of mourners—the *shendjetet*,[2] *djeret*,[3] and *matjeret*,[4] during the funerary service; they played harps, rattled *sistra*, swung clapsticks, sang as *meret*-singers,[5] and served as percussionists at royal funerals and cults; they served in the priestly offices of *ka-* or funerary priestess, priestess of Min, and "goddess's servants" of Khufu, Ptah, Neith, and Hathor; they performed services in the *Sed* Festival; and perhaps most tellingly for the role of women during this time, they were also accorded the titles of overseer of funerary priests of the king's mother, overseer of funerary priests, overseer of mourners, and overseer of the *shendjetet* or funerary dancers/offering givers. Women were placed as overseers of other women only, but they would have been responsible for superintending groups of priestesses and mourners. This involved duties that separated and elevated them from the majority, and gave them a social context that was higher even than many men.

CONCLUSION

There is an enormous amount of archaeological and literary material for Egyptian religion, many times more than for any other facet of their society, leading to the conclusion that the Egyptians were a strongly pious people. Despite this, however, it has been debated that they were in fact no more pious than certain people today. Judging the depth of ancient religious belief by artifactual evidence will inevitably leave gaps in modern understanding of that belief. It will always be colored by the fact that the evidence is being regarded in a twenty-first century context, at least 2000 years away in time from the living religion. Nevertheless, it is worthwhile to note that with the temple and the state so inextricably entwined, the position of the reigning king as Horus incarnate was inescapably both religious and political. He would, of necessity, have had to maintain both positions equally. One of the most obvious examples of his power and political supremacy was the monumental religious buildings. The pyramids, one of the cases in point, stand as not-so-subtle reminders of the colossal amount of human and other resources at the king's command, as well as serving as points from which the dead king might enter the afterlife. On a purely religious basis, these constructions, the largest buildings of stone yet erected by human labor, were tombs, meant to house a dead body and the accompanying grave goods. Anyone visiting the pyramids, however, cannot help but be struck by a strong, almost overwhelming feeling of overall exorbitance in material, labor, and vision. It is precisely that emotion that proclaimed the breadth and width of the king's power to the ancients.

NOTES

1. J. Baines, "Restricted Knowledge, Hierarchy and Decorum: Modern Perceptions and Ancient Institutions," *JARCE* 27 (1990): 1–23.

2. *Shendjet*-mourners were funerary dancers, giving offerings to the deceased.

3. *Djeret*-mourners seem to have been responsible for the wailing, or possibly the percussion that attended funerals in ancient Egypt. They are portrayed in the art as Isis and Nephthys, the divine mourners of Osiris' death.

4. The term *matjeret* is generally understood to mean a type of mourner, although not everyone agrees with this translation, and nothing is known of their duties, whether funerary or not.

5. A group of female singers led by a male director, sometimes known in the funerary texts as "the *meret*-singers of Upper and Lower Egypt."

CHAPTER 3

Symbolism of the Pyramids

The pyramid complexes and their ground plans provided potent symbolism for the ancient Egyptians, royal and commoner, that operated on both political and religious levels. As the largest man-made objects in the ancient Egyptian world, they were powerful reminders of the might of the kingship, reinforcing the right of the king to rule Egypt. As colossal stone tomb mounds, they took on, in architectural representation, the aspect of the primeval mound from Egyptian mythology, thereby aligning the dead king with the earliest deities and the beginning of the world. In terms of the living king, both the political and the religious meanings were significant because together, they gave his position on the throne a mythical underpinning, a structure that had profound consequences lasting the span of Egyptian history, namely the belief in the divinity of the king. In a state such as Egypt, the government of which mixed temple and state seamlessly and completely, the political and religious notions inherent in the pyramid complexes were inseparable. While the size and shape of the pyramid were symbols of both religious and political thought, the entire pyramid complex was an intrinsic part of that symbolism. This included decoration, which, before the end of the Fifth Dynasty, was not present in pyramids themselves, but found in the valley buildings, causeways, and mortuary temples, as well as the textual decoration of the Pyramid Texts in the late Old Kingdom.

The shape of the pyramids has come under some scrutiny from scholars, primarily concerning the reason for choosing what is essentially a triangle. At least three theories have been proposed, the first being that the pyramidal shape imitated the sun's rays as they streamed down from the sky. A second theory postulates that the pyramid was meant to point toward the heavens, the ultimate destination of the dead king, and acted as a staircase thereto. Finally, a third understanding of the choice of shape argues that the pyramid is meant to represent the mythological primeval hill. In fact, within the myth of the primeval mound, the other theories can be found in a metaphoric sense, the mound itself having risen toward the sky from the Nun, the primeval watery abyss, and the sun having been born from the mound to rise to its place in the heavens. A large part of the reason for speculation on this point lies in the apparently sudden change from completely hidden underground tombs to tombs that are visible from many miles away. It is generally accepted that such a change indicates a shift in religious perception, as well as a profound political shift. The exact nature of those shifts is lost, but it is possible to conjecture that the role of the king took on new significance, with substantially greater material and labor resources under his control.

Most archaeological evidence can be found in support of the third, the pyramid as representation of the primeval hill. Upon excavation, a First Dynasty mastaba, S3038, at Saqqara, belonging to an anonymous man who seems to have been the most important official in the government from the reign of Anedjib, the sixth ruler of that dynasty, was discovered to have had a tumulus constructed over the burial chamber and a superstructure then covering the whole. This tumulus was fashioned into a stepped construction with four equal sides. It is conceivable, even likely, that such a tumulus covered the burial chambers of the kings of the dynasty; however, in general, the tombs of the Early Dynastic kings at Abydos suffered from erosion, so it is not possible to know for certainty that tumuli were part of their tombs. In explaining the presence of this hidden mound, which covers the most vulnerable part of the tomb, from the perspective of the deceased, the mythological notion of a primeval mound seems to be particularly important. One of the earliest cosmogonic myths in Egypt was that of an original piece of earth arisen from the Nun, from which life first grew on earth. Redolent of the birth of the world and carrying within it a powerful regenerative force, this mound symbolically passed that particular force on to anything with which it became associated. Recreating the symbol of the primeval mound over the burial chamber of the tomb owner then lends potency and mythological force to the idea of being resurrected into the afterlife. The spiritual and symbolic strength of such an image would require that it be hidden from human eyes; hence, the need to cover a "primeval mound" with a layer of mudbrick or stone. To leave it open to sight would diminish its power, and potentially, unleash its inherent danger.

The next archaeological expression we see of the stepped construction over the burial chamber is Djoser's Step Pyramid and its complex at Saqqara, where the need for secrecy and concealment seems to have been overcome in quite a spectacular manner. It has recently been suggested that the reason for the jump in size lay in the desire to have the tomb visible from outside the enclosure wall, something it wouldn't have been otherwise. Originally, Djoser's tomb would have been a very large mastaba; however, sometime during its construction, he increased its proportions by adding another five ever-smaller mastabas on top of the first one. The appearance, as opposed to size, of this stepped superstructure above the burial chamber may be seen as a further interpretation of the primeval hill, although now, the hidden tumulus as a representation of the primeval hill was no longer too dangerous or sacred for the commoners. It had become an emblem of the king's wealth and power, taking on a political element, rather than being a completely religious symbol. The king was not hiding his association with primeval Egypt; he was placing himself on a par with it. He was declaring his connection with the beginnings of life in a mythological past, and using that connection to be reborn into the afterlife.

The largest representations of the connection of the king with the primeval hill and the afterlife were, of course, the pyramids at Giza, which proclaimed the king's strength, both political and religious, on a scale that has yet to be outdone. Subsequently, every pyramid constructed made use of the same primeval symbolism and proclamation of power, and every pyramid except Khufu's was constructed using the same basic plan with various and generally, symbolically inconsequential variations. Most importantly, with the exception of the pyramid of Khufu, the burial chambers were located under the ground level of the pyramids in the center. They were thus in a similar position to the burial chambers under the hidden tumuli in the Early Dynastic royal burials. Khufu's burial chamber, however, was in the middle of the pyramid itself. It was a much more difficult engineering feat to incorporate a chamber into the body of the pyramid than it was to build a pyramid over a chamber set into the foundational rock, and the fact that Khufu's pyramid was the first built on the Giza Plateau needs to be kept in mind. It seems likely that the engineering involved was too time-consuming and difficult to arrange, and thus, this architectural accomplishment was never repeated.

Placing the burial chamber in the center of the pyramid was also a symbolic gesture. The king's dead body, and the other portions of his spiritual body, were surrounded by the emblematic primeval hill, not simply under it, and this had the symbolic effect of making the king a part of the representation of original earth, rather than having risen from it. This may have been an important distinction in the eyes of the Egyptians; the king was presenting himself, and his rebirth, as having been something that was intimately associated with the birth of the earth, before the existence of any other life, and not subsequent to the emergence of the primeval hill. This represents a further mythological step toward the idea, prevalent in the Old Kingdom, of the divine nature of the king, which began to appear in the Early Dynastic Period with the tumuli over the burial chambers of the kings and important commoners.

The interior walls of the mortuary temples of the Old Kingdom from the reign of Khufu, however, are decorated with what seems to be a fairly standard program of reliefs, some painted, some sculpted, and the general architecture of the later buildings appears to have reached a higher, more intricate level, both in terms of number of rooms and universal plan, as well as in the types of materials used in production. The reliefs consisted of a number of different scenes, which seem, from remaining fragments, to have been relatively similar in other causeways. Primarily, the subject matter was scenes of daily life, the final product of which activity was meant for the king. This included agricultural events of different kinds, offering-bearers with provisions of every kind, from exotic animals to great piles of bread. Also included were more warlike scenes, and scenes of hunting. Specific to Unas' causeway, perhaps because other causeways' examples were destroyed, are scenes of famine victims, emaciated and dying. Despite being part of the funerary complex of the pyramid, these reliefs are concerned with the mundane world from which the king has departed; they portray events that are specific to the life of the palace and the court, and, by extension, Egypt.

This stands in particular contrast with the Pyramid Texts, introduced in Unas' pyramid. They were intended specifically for the king to enter the afterlife, and as such, dealt with the spiritual or supernatural world, rather than the temporal world of the causeway reliefs. Offering texts comprise part of the corpus, but they involve the food offered, for the most part, during the interment of the body in the burial chamber; hence, the fleshless sustenance of the afterlife. This difference in textual context is extremely important in light of the symbolism of the pyramid complex as a whole. It highlights the significance of the pyramid as an area that was sacred space, meant for the king only. The causeway, although accessible only to priests, was less sacred and more mundane, where the earthly activities necessary for keeping up the funerary cult of the deceased king took place, including transportation of offering goods and personnel from the valley temple. As the avenue up which the embalmed body of the king was taken, it maintained a connection with the sacred space of the pyramid, while at the same time, became a crucial mundane link with the "outside" world.

With the exception of the Pyramid Texts, the elements of the pyramid complexes—the temples, chambers, enclosure walls, passageways—all had antecedents in the funerary complexes of the First and Second Dynasty kings. A line of architectural and symbolic development, involving these elements can be traced through the royal and élite tombs of the Early Dynastic Period at Abydos and Saqqara to the great pyramids of the Fourth Dynasty. The royal tombs at Abydos were located at Umm el Qaab, near the high desert, while their enclosure walls were erected approximately one mile further to the east, toward the Nile. It is possible that this was done to try to ensure the secrecy of the tomb's location and the grave goods that accompanied the king's body; despite this distance, however, the two elements constituted a funerary complex, the initial appearance of this type of mortuary architecture.

The wall itself was constructed using a "palace façade" style of architectural decoration, a regular series of indentations, possibly stylized crenellations, along the wall, in imitation of the royal palaces of the period. The area within the enclosure walls of the first two dynasties was used in the religious rites of the cult of the recently deceased king. The entrance to these enclosures was always along the eastern wall near the southeast corner, and within the walls, the cult buildings, one small building in each enclosure, were located in the southeast corner. The wall around the Step Pyramid complex, the next step toward the full development of the pyramid complex, was built in exactly this manner, although this complex contained a much greater ritualistic scope.

The cult buildings, the only architectural feature within the earliest enclosure walls, appear to have been the center of the funerary rituals, with what seem to have been burnt offerings of some kind, whether incense or something more substantial. According to the archaeological evidence from the earliest complexes, the rituals were conducted for some years after the death of the king, indicating that the cults were important elements of the religious worship of the period.

The symbolism connected to the location of the temple on a pyramid's east side lies in the direction of the rising sun. The eastern side of the pyramid and the entrance to the mortuary temple faced the rising sun, and were the first to be lit by the sun's nascent rays. For the Egyptians, the continued cycle of day and night, the rising and setting of the sun, was by no means certain, and could only be assured by the regular performance of specific diurnal and nocturnal rituals in the country's temples. The temples dedicated to deities, throughout the country, were built specifically to keep the world in natural working order, and it was believed that without the precise performance of certain rituals the world would fall into disarray and chaos.

VALLEY TEMPLES

A good number of the valley temples have not been excavated, usually because they lie under presently inhabited villages. The two best-preserved of the valley buildings are those belonging to Sneferu (the Bent Pyramid at Dahshur) and Khafre at Giza, both of the Fourth Dynasty. Khafre's valley temple is without relief on the inner walls of the building's chambers; however, the Bent Pyramid's valley building and what remains of those with more than simply floor plans and foundations, in particular Sahure's and Pepi II's, indicate that they were decorated with painted relief. The floor plans of the buildings were similar, with a T-shaped chapel, storage rooms, and entrance halls. The valley temples seem to have been located on a waterway, either a canal or the Nile itself, probably for practical as well as mythological reasons. The Nile was the life's blood of Egypt, and as a mythological symbol, it shared preeminence with the sun. The flow of the water was seen as the giver of life, and had its counterpart in the sky. The king's last voyage down the Nile to the valley temple, the first stage of his journey to the afterlife, was symbolic of his final place of being, in the boat of the sun, sailing the river of the sky. The valley buildings, then, represented the end of one voyage and the beginning of another.

The use to which the valley buildings were put is something of a mystery. It has been suggested that that was the place where the rituals for embalming took place, and possibly where the actual embalming was performed, although this suggestion has not met with universal agreement. Khafre's valley building has a courtyard on the roof, a feature found on most temples in Egypt, an area usually used for nocturnal rituals. In the case of Khafre's building, there are runnels from the rooftop courtyard leading to the chambers below, indicating perhaps that fluid was meant to travel down them. The T-shaped chapel was likely the most important room in the building, and it housed a number of statues of the king, as many as twenty-three in the case of Khafre's building, judging from the remaining plinths. What is assumed to be one of these statues, a diorite-gneiss larger-than-life-sized seated statue of Khafre, now in the Cairo Museum, was found in a pit in the antechamber of the valley building. The quality of workmanship on this statue is surpassed only by the four slate statues of Menkaure with two goddesses, found in the excavation of his valley building (see Document 2). The fact of their incomparable quality together with their mere presence is an indication of the important position of the building in the symbolism of the pyramid complex as a whole. The meaning invested in the statues is unknown, but it seems likely that they were of primary significance to the entire ritual procedure, both during the rituals of burying the king and those held for his funerary cult thereafter.

PYRAMID TEXTS

The Pyramid Texts were also a part of the symbolic nature of the pyramids, providing the dead king with the wherewithal to reach his divine ancestors and surrounding him with the magical properties the hieroglyphs maintained in a religious context. They were a series of hieroglyphic "Utterances" or spells written on the walls of the late Old Kingdom pyramids, beginning with Unas, last king of the Fifth Dynasty (see Documents 12–17). They were inscribed on the entranceway walls, in the antechamber, and in the burial chamber. The only walls not inscribed were those of the serdab, or statue room, which were anepigraphic. The texts were intended to aid the king skyward, to help in his ascent into the company of the gods, and it is generally assumed that the texts were for the use of the king only, largely because they have not been found in anything but a royal context. The first occurrence of a Pyramid Text outside the walls of the pyramid was during the reign of Pepi I, in an inscription on a libation table in his mortuary temple.

The texts themselves are not numbered in Egyptian, although they have been put into a modern numerical order from the entrance corridors into the burial chambers. The number of texts is approximately 759, but that number is still growing, as more are discovered with further excavation. Some of them indicate a very early origin for the Pyramid Text group as a whole, by referring to the burial of bodies directly into the sand, with further accoutrements, and some of the texts can be found verbatim in the corpus of Coffin Texts, a later group of funerary texts. Mistakes in the writing of certain portions of the grammar and in the hieroglyphic spelling of some words indicate that the texts were carved into the walls from papyrus copies misread by the scribes. Almost every spell begins with the phrase, "Words to be spoken," and this has led to the term "Utterance" being used by modern scholars to indicate a new texts.

There is some question as to which way the texts were intended to be read and thus ordered, from the entranceway texts in to the burial chamber texts, or the other way around. The reasoning for reading them from the outside into the burial chamber lies in the notion of the recitation of the texts during the king's interment. Reading the texts from the inside out lies with the texts' use by the dead king. It does not appear, however, that the texts were intended to be read in a linear order, but rather, they seem to have been intended to work in an interconnected kind of manner, making use of the architecture and space of the chambers. Certain types of texts are grouped together; for example, those around the vulnerable entrances to the rooms tend to be prophylactic and protection spells against both mundane dangers, such as snakes and scorpions, and supernatural dangers, such as evil spirits and demons. The spells around the sarcophagus in the burial chamber were devoted to the various offerings necessary for the king. It has been postulated that the spells move, in content, toward the serdab, and that the serdab is the ultimate end, a metaphorical sky. The serdab is left without texts of any kind because there is no need for them, once the "sky" has been reached.

It is important to keep in mind that once the funeral procession had occurred, the king placed in the sarcophagus, and the offerings stored, the portcullises were let down and the entire structure sealed, ostensibly for all eternity. Who, then, was meant to read the Pyramid Texts? All evidence suggests they were never meant to be seen again, at least by living eyes. It seems most likely that they were intended for the dead king's use in the afterlife, and in the end, the textual, artistic, and architectural elements acted with one accord to invest the sum of the parts with a representational understanding of the royal afterlife.

Once the king died, his supernatural life was spent in the exalted company of the gods. While superficially appearing to be similar to the commoners' topography, in fact the royal supernatural geography during the Old Kingdom was much less defined than the commoner's geographical afterlife. The royal landscape was a watery one, with reed marshes and river banks. The sky was the river being described, often called the Winding Waterway and associated with the Milky Way. The banks of the celestial river were the horizons of the earth, likely to the north and the south. There were also several fields or marshes named in the Texts, one such being the Field of Reeds. The sky river had the same kinds of eddies and flows, marshy areas, and riverine traffic that the Nile had, and naturally, the sun and the moon would cross from east to west in boats crewed by the divine inhabitants.

CONCLUSION

The purpose of the pyramid complex was manifold. It served in the first place as a series of elements functioning simultaneously in a symbolic manner to convey the king into the afterlife by means of his funeral and funerary rites. After this was accomplished, the continued presence and use of the complex was intended to work toward keeping the king in the afterlife. All the rituals that were enacted on each day in the mortuary temple were integral contributions to the way in which the complexes were intended to serve the needs of the mortuary cult of the king. The pyramid texts in the late Old Kingdom were textual assurance of the royal ascent to the sky and the continued presence of the king (and Pepi I's queens) in the ancestral company. This presence was vital for Egypt as a whole, on a symbolic level, ensuring that the position of the country and its people would be maintained in their world view, and would not fall to chaos or overthrow by outside influences. Each portion of the complex, then, assisted in the ultimate symbolic goal of ensuring the existence of Egypt on a cosmic scale in the universe, and generally, its hegemony in their known ancient world.

CHAPTER 4

THE WHERE AND HOW OF PYRAMID BUILDING

LOCATION, LOCATION, LOCATION

An important decision for both the king and his architectural advisors regarding the construction of the pyramids was the choice of a pyramid's location. The earliest Egyptians maintained settlements at a limited number of sites; in the area of Middle Egypt from approximately Hierakonpolis to Abydos, at the apex of the Delta, and at various sites in the Delta itself. With the unification of Egypt during Dynasty Zero, Memphis was the capital and royal residence, and the most important political center in the newly fashioned country. Close to the apex of the Delta, it was a vital location for establishing a firm royal presence and relationship with the north. Tombs of royal courtiers from the reign of Ka, the predecessor of Narmer, were built both at Saqqara, on the escarpment of the high desert just above Memphis, and at nearby Helwan, on the other side of the river. Despite the institution of an élite necropolis, however, the tombs of the earliest kings were located at Abydos and Umm el-Gaab in Middle Egypt, a considerable distance from the capital.

Abydos was close to Hierakonpolis, the major predynastic and Early Dynastic center in the south, and one that had ties with the oases and the nomadic peoples in Nubia. Perhaps as a result of the proximity to such a key site, Abydos was chosen as the royal necropolis of the earliest kings to ensure an ongoing presence in the area. This made Abydos as important a location, symbolically, as Memphis, at least for the First Dynasty. With the advent of the Second Dynasty, this changed, and for all intents and purposes, the royal necropolis moved from Abydos to Saqqara. With the exception of the last two kings of Dynasty Two, and until Dynasty Eighteen, Egyptian kings were buried around Memphis in the necropolis field that stretched from Abu Roash in the north to Meidum and Hawara in the south.

Each pyramid along the west bank was visible to the others, creating a long line of royal tomb markers. While the various fields are now discussed in terms of separate necropoli, it seems that the entire area was considered to be one great burial ground by the Egyptians, with no distinctions between, for example, Giza and Saqqara, or any of the other sites. It is important to keep in mind that all the fields were within sight of Memphis, providing daunting reminders of royal power for the ancient Egyptians, even after the rulers' deaths. Memphis, as the royal city, was the most important settlement in Old Kingdom Egypt, and its location at the juncture of Upper and Lower Egypt was the crux. In cultural terms, the towns and settlement sites of Lower Egypt were independent both from each other and from those in Upper Egypt. Upper Egyptian settlements show a certain amount of cultural similarity and progression across the entire area, whereas settlements in Lower Egypt seem to have been culturally and economically independent. Politically, it was imperative to maintain control over both areas simultaneously, and part of the process of instituting control was the assertion of power, even in death.

Several moves from site to site along this pyramid field corridor were apparently due to changes in religious beliefs; the move by Djedefre, son of Khufu, of his pyramid site to Abu Roash from Giza could be interpreted as a desire to be more directly west of Heliopolis, the city of the sun, and the most important religious center in the country. Other changes of site may be attributed to more pragmatic reasons; the Giza Plateau had run out of space by the end of the Fourth Dynasty, meaning a move for the funerary space of the Fifth Dynasty was an inevitable necessity. At the same time, the focus of the religion seemed to change during the Fifth Dynasty, and sun cults and temples were introduced into the funerary complexes. An obligatory shift in location may, then, have been not unwelcome and even, perhaps, serendipitous to take advantage of the institution of a new development of funerary style.

The choice of the desert plateau for the early establishment of royal necropoli was likely a multifaceted one: the desert was not arable, and, therefore, building the mastabas and pyramids of the royals on it did not use invaluable agricultural land. The desert edges were often near prime quarrying possibilities, which was one of the most important pragmatic considerations. This was, in fact, probably one of the deciding factors for choice of site, as the closer the source for the stone, the quicker the work could proceed without having to haul the stone or float it down river from further-flung sites, both time- and energy-consuming tasks. The desert also had the advantage of height, giving it visibility, and seclusion, keeping it away from the living. Even today, the mastabas and pyramids along the high desert plateau edge make a very strong visual statement; in the third millennium B.C.E., with the original casings on the structures and the ever-encroaching sand kept at bay, the sight would have struck exactly the right note in inspiring awe.

THE ORGANIZATION OF MANPOWER

The construction of the pyramids was a complicated and bureaucratically tangled undertaking. The manpower required was staggering, and included not only the backbreaking task of quarrying and hauling the stones, but also the skills of the architect (like Imhotep, the legendary architect of Djoser), artists, engineers, and all the positions in-between, such as overseers, food preparers, scribes of all levels, etc. The Egyptians used a system of forced labor called a corvée. This method of acquiring a work force required every subject to contribute a certain amount of unpaid labor to be given to the state each year. This type of labor system is possible only with a well-established census of population, something the Egyptians had had since the beginning of the unification of Upper and Lower Egypt, and without which, it would be difficult, if not impossible, to ascertain the size of the labor pool from which to pull the workforce. Theoretically, every citizen in the land was subject to this conscription of labor; however, it was within the prerogative of the king to exempt certain classes and groups of people from participation. Textual evidence supports this, showing that those in the higher economic levels were often royally exempted from work in the corvée. As a result, it was primarily the people without such royal means, the farmers and laborers, who were at the royal beck and call, although the state did use skilled labor and artisans in the corvée, as well.

The work was necessarily done throughout the year, rather than only during the summer, the period of the Nile's inundation, during which agriculture was impossible. As the period of inundation—July to September— was the hottest during the year in Egypt, it was not the ideal time for heavy labor, and it seems likely that less work could have been accomplished during this period than any other throughout the year. Another argument for the year-long construction activity lies in the number of laborers the various pyramid fields could accommodate. The largest number of workmen was undoubtedly used for the construction of the pyramids at Giza, the Great Pyramid in particular. Numbers proposed by scholars and historians for building Khufu's pyramid range from 10,000 to 100,000 workmen at any one time. Feasibility studies on the plateau itself and the rate of work suggest that the most realistic number lies in the presence of 20,000 to 30,000 workmen on the plateau, the hard laborers working in rotating gangs throughout the year, like for periods of three months at a time, and the more skilled workmen—the artisans, stone-working specialists, and others—laboring year round.

The work of the divisions on the pyramids and their complexes was divided by the cardinal directions of north and south or east and west; thus, the buildings were built by two teams of workers working side by side, one of which assembled on one half of the building, while the second assembled the other half. The workmen left their marks, called mason's marks, on each block of every construction; some archaeologists believe that every block in the great Giza pyramids has a mason's mark on them. These marks helped with tallying the work done daily by each crew, and they provide invaluable evidence for the methods of construction. Two buildings in particular supply names and positions—the relieving chambers in the pyramid of Khufu and the mortuary temple of Menkaure.

The relieving chambers in Khufu's pyramid are a series of five intentional cavities separated by five immense blocks of stone, culminating with an apex, above the ceiling of the funerary chamber of the king. The cavities themselves allow a person of average height to stand almost to full height, and their purpose was to distribute and alleviate the immense weight of the rest of the pyramid above.

Mason's marks have been found on the side walls of the cavities that indicate the method in which the blocks were set into place. The inner blocks of the mortuary temple of Menkaure, visible due to the depredation of the building, show four phyles, or divisions, working side by side in groups of two. They appear to have belonged to two separate gangs, rather than belonging to the same gang. The names of the gangs are typical of the period: the Drunks of Menkaure and the Companions of Menkaure. The Companions of Menkaure left their marks on the southern blocks of the building, while the Drunks left theirs on the northern blocks, indicating that each gang and its accompanying phyles were responsible for the hauling of the blocks and their positioning, similar to the work done on Khufu's relieving chambers. It is conceivable that the gangs were also responsible for the quarrying of the blocks, as it is evident from stratigraphy in the stone itself that the blocks were hewn at the same time from the same place in the quarry.

METHODS OF CONSTRUCTION

Preparing the Ground

Having chosen the site, the first task was leveling the ground, to create both the pyramid area and a courtyard surrounding it. It was imperative that the pyramid blocks themselves be equally level from the ground up to prevent (probably exponentially) severe engineering mistakes higher in the pyramid's construction, and this was ultimately more important than ensuring that the courtyard was level. The leveling of the courtyard was a task that could see, as in the case of Khafre's pyramid on the Giza Plateau, the removal of approximately 33 feet of limestone from the plateau in the northeast corner took place. Despite the removal of this quite astonishing amount of bedrock, it was still necessary to shore up the opposite corner with huge foundation blocks. The leveling of this pyramid/courtyard area was accomplished by using a square level, which consisted of a triangle on two wooden legs of the same length with a plumb-bob hanging from the apex of the triangle. The levels taken by this instrument were likely marked on the stone walls left after excavating to the courtyard level, as has been found at a mastaba at Meidum. These marks provided the engineers and architects with stable and accurate indications from which to measure the first courses of the pyramid; higher than that, however, it is unknown how a precisely level surface was achieved.

Another unknown feature is how the first course of blocks and the corner blocks in particular were laid in place so as to provide accurate guidelines for the rest of the measurements. Directional orientations could have been taken by the stars or the sun, using one of several methods. The most likely seems to have been a gnomon, like that on a sundial. In order to make the shadow sharp, another instrument was used to define the edges, making the measurement as precise as possible. Another possible method was using a circle bisected by the shadows of a gnomon in the morning and the afternoon. The line would be taken between the two points and that line itself bisected, the point of bisection giving north. The precision with which the pyramids at Giza, in particular, were made has been well-attested, the measurements of the cardinal directions being to within one degree of accuracy or less, indicating the efficacy of whichever method was used.

Pyramids that have collapsed, as in the later, mudbrick-centered pyramids of the Twelfth Dynasty, and pyramids that were never finished show that the interiors of those pyramids (and likely most others) for the initial layers generally either used outcroppings of stone left to stabilize the entire construction or used skeleton walls within to create chambers into which rubble and debris were thrown, again to provide stability as well as to cut down on the number of interior stone blocks. This method can be seen in the Fifth Dynasty pyramid of Niuserre at Abusir, and in the Twelfth Dynasty pyramids of Senwosret I, Amenemhat II, and Senwosret II. As earlier pyramids, those of the Fourth Dynasty in particular, are still standing, it is impossible to do other than conjecture that they were built using the same foundational techniques. In some of the pyramids of the Fifth Dynasty, the cores appear to have been stepped, while those of the Fourth Dynasty appear to have been built in inclining layers. It is unfortunate that until the destruction of a Fourth Dynasty pyramid, this question will remain unanswered.

Quarrying and Hauling the Stones

The work of quarrying and hauling, at its simplest form, involved the following procedures. First, the blocks of stone had to be quarried. There were several methods of doing this, using copper, stone, and wood tools, although the precise nature of these is not known. It is likely that quarrying the stone blocks from the living rock was done with stone tools, probably picks or axes. The size of the block was measured and indicated on the top of the bedrock and then, the work of removing a channel on all sides began. Hard rock, such as granite and basalt, took much longer to hew from the ground than softer stone, such as limestone or sandstone. Once the channels had been dug slightly below the desired level of the bottom of the block, runnels were cut into the stone below the block. These runnels or trenchs were then filled with water and wooden logs were placed in them. As the wood soaked up the water, it expanded and pushed the block up from its crude pedestal.

Having thus quarried out the block, it was transported to the working level to be maneuvered into place. Blocks of limestone and sandstone were not dressed until they reached the site and were ready for final placement. Dressing the softer stones was left to specialists at the various pyramid sites. Blocks of granite or basalt, however, were dressed at the quarry and transported in a completed state, indicating that the finishers of these particular stones stayed at the quarrying site. The hauling was done by men and oxen pulling the blocks on sleds and, likely, water to dampen the sand for ease of movement. The pyramids were generally sited close to good limestone quarrying sites, thus limiting the distance necessary for hauling; however, certain parts of the pyramids, such as the granite slabs in the burial chamber of Khufu's pyramid required hauling of great distances.

The granite quarries used during the Old Kingdom were situated in Aswan and the blocks quarried therefrom were too heavy for riverine transport. As a result, they had to be hauled by hand to Giza, a distance of over 435 miles. It is perhaps no surprise that the harder stones were limited to a few particular uses, where weight-bearing was an essential factor, as in Khufu's burial chamber, or when the design required a specific material, such as the paving of the pyramid temple of Khufu.

Ramps

The blocks were dragged up to the working level of the pyramid by means of ramps made using cast-off materials from the larger construction. Remains of short ramps have been discovered against the sides of unfinished pyramids; not surprisingly, each is constructed differently of varying materials according to the size and material of the pyramid. Generally, the bulk of the ramp was made up of the limestone and other stone chips that littered the grounds as a result of finishing the blocks to be used in the pyramid. The sides were shored up in some way, by bricks or larger stones, and sand and mortar were used to compact the chips into a solid rising platform.

The question of how the longer and higher ramps went up the sides of the pyramids has not been answered in a satisfactory manner. There are at least four probable types of ramp that may have been used; the linear ramp going straight up one side of the pyramid, the spiral ramp ascending around all four sides of the pyramid, the interior ramp going up through the middle of the pyramid, and the staircase ramp, going in zig-zag fashion up one side of the pyramid. The linear ramp has three variations: a wide ramp in the earlier stages with sides sloping down to the outer edges of the pyramid's sides that becomes narrower the higher it climbs, a narrow ramp with wider sides, or a narrow ramp with straight sides. This last seems, of all three types, to be the least tenable, as it would be the least stable and the most difficult to maintain.

The type most likely to have been used on a fairly regular basis, keeping in mind that it is probable that few pyramid constructions were done with precisely the same kind of ramp as any other, was the interior ramp. Running up through the center of the pyramid, this provided the sides of the ramp with a built-in stabilizer, that is the growing pyramid, and made the ramp less steep, easing the downward slope and accompanying pull of gravity. It has been estimated by modern experimentation that on slopes the number of men needed to pull one block would increase considerably. From two men hauling a 5 to 6 ton block on the flat, the number needed would rise to nine on a slope of 9 degrees. This would also have an effect on the type of ramp used. It would be substantially more dangerous to have a steep, thin ramp than one with a wider and more gentle slope. The ramp that has the gentlest slope is the interior ramp, making it the most likely.

Pyramid Construction

Once the blocks had been moved to the working level of the pyramid, the sides were finished and they were set into place. The interior blocks were not as finely finished as the outer blocks, there being no aesthetic reason for doing so, and time and manpower were undoubtedly better used finishing what could be seen. The fitting of the outer blocks was of much greater importance, and had to be mathematically precise in order not to skew the final result. Incorrect measurements and miscalculations were responsible for the Bent Pyramid. Although the mistakes made on the Bent Pyramid were ones of miscalculating the incline and not of keeping the corners straight, the pyramid was nonetheless visible as a reminder that perfection was the goal.

With the placing of the outer blocks comes the question of whether they were placed from the middle out to the corners or from the corners in toward the center. Either method had the potential for difficulties with inaccurate calculations; it appears, however, that the blocks were maneuvered from the sides, rather than from the front or back, indicating that the placement technique used was from the middle out to the edges. Levers were used to move the blocks into place, and many blocks show evidence of notches for such a use. Ropes were also used, but only for the movement of blocks within the pyramid's chambers, when it was necessary to slide them in a controlled manner down inclined passageways.

Perhaps the most difficult engineering feats were the inclusion of passageways and chambers within the pyramids. The earliest pyramids show some attempts to raise the burial and other chambers above ground level, but it wasn't until Khufu's pyramid that the chambers were included in the body of the pyramid. Ensuring that the burial and other chambers were aligned according to the cardinal directions was one of the challenges facing the architects. The most likely method was the simultaneous construction of the above-ground chambers with the surrounding masonry. The orientation would have been relatively easy to calculate in these instances, and the entrance passages slightly easier to construct. When the chambers were below ground, however, the task became more difficult and without compasses or even sightlines, how they managed to align the chambers with such accuracy is unknown.

The roofing of the chambers was one of three types: the corbelled roof, the flat roof, and the pointed roof. The use of roofing type depended upon the surrounding structure. The corbelled roof was created by projecting each succeeding ascending course of blocks over the lower one until the blocks are close enough at the top to be sealed by one or two blocks alone. This type of roofing relieves the pressure from the top by redirecting it down the sides of the chambers. The earliest corbelling was done in the pyramid at Meidum, but continued being used in the pyramids at Dahshur as well as Giza; the most famous example is in the gallery in Khufu's pyramid. This pyramid also contained an example of the pointed and the flat roofs, in the king's burial chamber. The roof of the chamber itself is flat, but the ancient engineers added five small chambers on top, each of which had a floor and ceiling composed of long stone blocks, with the exception of the fifth, which had a pointed roof. It seems likely that these so-called relieving chambers were intended to deflect the weight from above, much the same as the corbelled roof did in the Meidum pyramid.

The last block to be maneuvered into position was the capstone, or pyramidion. This was likely the most difficult task of the entire building project, for a number of reasons. It would require some sort of levering mechanism to move it into its final place, and that task itself entailed a specialized manpower and a relatively small area in which to work. It was also the highest block on the pyramid, and, hence, the farthest to haul upward. It appears, as well, that by this time, the internal ramp would have to have been filled in, as the working space at the top of the pyramid would have been simply too small for the maneuvering required for capstone placement. With the internal ramp filled in, lifting the capstone was done either by dragging the stone up the side of the pyramid, or by creating a series of lifts.

The final additions to the pyramids were the fine limestone outer casings and the finishing. The lower courses of Menkaure's pyramid show that it was not finished by the time of the king's death, as the smoothing of the outer limestone blocks was never completed. This unfinished state allows us the opportunity to see what is essentially a work-in-progress; it is apparent that the blocks were set into place before they were finished, and they were all finished together, rather than one at a time. This was probably both a time-saving measure and a method that enabled the stonecutters to work more efficiently as a team across one face of the pyramid, rather than one block at a time.

The fortunate wealth of archaeological evidence on the Giza Plateau has left a reasonably complete picture of how the pyramids were built, at least those on the plateau itself. It is extremely likely, if not probable, that each pyramid's construction varied in numerous ways; there is evidence, for example, that the ramps up the sides of the pyramids were constructed using different materials and different ascending routes with each pyramid. This should be expected, as each pyramid was constructed as a unique entity, and not one of a series. The available evidence has also left strong indications of the amount of engineering and labor that was required, as well as the depth of scientific knowledge that the Egyptians had available to them. The pyramids stand as mute testimony to the ingenuity, determination, and achievements of the ancient engineer.

CHAPTER 5

THE PYRAMID BUILDERS

It is axiomatic that the pyramids could not have been built without the labor of thousands of workers of all kinds—from architects and engineers to quarriers and stone-haulers, from cooks and textile workers to food preparers and laundry workers. The image of thousands of toiling, hard-used laborers hauling gigantic blocks of stone in the cruel Egyptian sun have filled the minds and movie-screens of the world, from Herodotus, the Greek historian of the fifth century B.C.E. who traveled around the ancient world compiling his Histories, until the present day with the Biblical epics of Hollywood. Such images have influenced the popular imagination and led to often wildly unrealistic notions of the harshness of Egyptian taskmasters and the brutal, short lives of the builders.

The reality of the work environment on the various pyramid sites was likely to be neither as harsh nor as crowded as is generally believed. The Egyptians were nothing if not pragmatic, and archaeological evidence indicates they were aware of the benefits of not working their laborers to death. The hard laborers were not the only servants of the state involved with the construction of the pyramids: a group of workers often overlooked, perhaps because of their archaeological silence, are what might be termed "support staff," or those men and women responsible for directly feeding and clothing the hard laborers. The state fed, clothed, and housed the workmen and the support staff, with varying degrees of comfort, and ensured that the work was rotational to make the best possible use of the country's labor force.

PYRAMID TOWNS

There is archaeological evidence at all the pyramid fields—Giza, Abusir, Saqqara, Dahshur, and Meidum—of pyramid towns, settlements built specifically for the workmen, and later used to house the personnel associated with the running of the pyramid temples' cults. Sometimes these settlements lasted for hundreds of years; the pyramid town associated with the Fourth Dynasty pyramid of Menkaure on the Giza Plateau was inhabited until the end of the Sixth Dynasty, more than 300 years later. With other rulers, however, they were abandoned after the construction of the pyramid complexes; the buildings at many of the pyramid fields that are possibly the remains of pyramid towns appear to have suffered this fate, the town at Dahshur having been not only abandoned, but then intentionally destroyed and razed.

The earliest pyramid towns, likely all contemporary, were those at Meidum and Dahshur belonging to Sneferu, first king of Dynasty Four. The remains at Meidum are relatively vast, and show a habitation site that was larger than any other in the Old Kingdom. As with the later towns at other pyramid sites, the town at Meidum was populated with workers in the cult of the king, including priests, guards, scribes, and other functionaries. The inhabitants were descendants of the original residents who were distant relations of the king, and therefore of royal blood. The appointment of royal relatives to positions in pyramid towns seems to have been a measure to ensure the ongoing practice of the royal and other funerary cults.

The identification of the remains at both Giza and Dahshur as those of pyramid towns is very tentative. Primarily they consist of the scant remains of what appear to have been buildings that housed the living, as opposed to mortuary architecture; there are two at Dahshur and one at Saqqara. Other than these sparse archaeological indications, the evidence for pyramid towns at Dahshur is purely textual, in the form of a decree dated to the Sixth Dynasty reign of Pepi I set up as a record of the rights that accompanied the royal privilege of living in the two pyramid towns associated with the two pyramids of Sneferu at the site, the Red (or north) and the Bent (or south) Pyramids (see Documents 6 and 8 for a similar text from the reign of Pepi II). The text indicates that the two towns, despite being several miles apart, were administered as one unit, and that the valley temples were the centers of the administration. It also states specifically that it was erected to restrict abuses of the system. As one of the rights of those working for the valley temples or in the pyramid towns was exemption from the corvée and others involved exemption from taxes, and rights to revenue from royal donations, abuses were no doubt frequent, expensive, and quite possibly deleterious to the economic stability of the area. It is likely that the inhabitants of the towns, a limited number according to the stela, were of the highest ranking religious officials, and comprised a group related, albeit tangentially, to the king, given that the privileges of living in the pyramid towns were lucrative and involved the personal involvement of the king.

Giza Pyramid Towns

The only evidence for the use of such towns during the building of a pyramid is found at Giza. There, excavations south of the plateau have uncovered what appears to be a large industrial complex, surrounded by an enclosure wall with a gate in the west end, that was used for the preparation of large quantities of food and drink, as well as areas for copper workshops and storerooms. Part of this complex included several sleeping areas, likely for the buildings' workers. The extent of the complex is vast, running 246 feet along the north/south axis and at least 170 feet, 7 inches along the east/west axis, indicating an operation that catered to an equally immense number of people. The space was divided into long narrow rooms, built of mudbrick, called galleries by the excavator. These galleries were approximately 114 feet, 10 inches long and 16 feet, 5 inches wide, and accommodated work and sleep areas. They were arranged in long rows of eight side by side, facing another row of eight approximately 16 feet, 5 inches away across a paved corridor. This corridor is perhaps the earliest example of pavement in the world, and is composed of limestone gravel covered by densely packed mud, with a trough down the middle that worked as a drain. The food production areas include a large number of bakeries, breweries, kitchens, and what appears to have been a fish processing area. Often sleeping areas are in close vicinity to the food production areas, leaving the impression that they were intended specifically for workers on the job.

A layer excavated to the southeast of the Giza Plateau seems to have been what may be the rest of a workers' installation. Textual evidence for the pyramid towns of Khufu and Khafre, which may indeed be these southern complexes, indicates that they were established on a small scale during the early Fourth Dynasty, and were initially administered by a son of the king. Expansion occurred during the Fifth Dynasty, as in the pyramid town of Menkaure, discussed below.

Just north of the southernmost complex and separating it from the plateau proper is a massive stone wall, known as the Heit el Ghourab, or Wall of the Crow. The wall itself is more than 33 feet thick, and the gate is approximately 8 feet in breadth and 23 feet high. The monumental size of the gateway seems to indicate that it was intended to serve as a primary, or perhaps even a royal, entrance to the Giza Plateau, accommodating perhaps as many as five men abreast. It was discovered that the wall formed a distinct part of the complex and appeared to provide the back wall of galleries abutting it, making it an integral portion of the complex. Whether the complex was enlarged at some point, making the wall the furthest north for possible additions and hence, a time-saving use of a preexisting construction, or whether the wall was included in the original plans for construction is unknown, but such a question can, and likely will, be solved by further excavation and analysis.

The reason for this wall is unknown, but it has been suggested that it may have been the entrance to the Giza Plateau or perhaps worked to deflect flood waters that would occasionally come down the wadi in which the complex was situated. Most likely, it served in both capacities; it was thick enough at 33 feet wide and high enough at over 23 feet to withstand the sudden, very damaging floods occasioned by desert rainstorms, and the same properties would provide the necessary enclosure for the sacred space of the plateau. The size and monumentality of the wall, not to mention the stone construction material, were ideally suited to provide the sense of exclusivity required to keep the pyramid area sacrosanct.

The pyramid town excavated to the southwest of the pyramid of Menkaure was a completely different matter. To all appearances, the town was not enclosed by a wall, in the way the southern complex was. The fact of its situation without the boundaries of the Wall of the Crow might indicate that the southern complex had served its purpose and was no longer in use. It also appears to have grown organically after the interment of Menkaure, during the period of royal cultic activity at the mortuary and valley temples. Originally, it seemed to have been organized around Menkaure's valley temple; however, by the late Fifth Dynasty, the area of habitation had spread to the courtyard of the valley temple, leaving only the cult rooms unoccupied. The excavator cleared fifteen units that were scattered in the area, each of which had four to eight rooms of varying sizes. As with the rooms in the southern complex, most (although not all) of these units seemed to have been primarily for industrial activity of some kind, including bakeries or kitchens. Other units appeared habitable, perhaps providing areas for the workers to rest during periods of inactivity or houses for members of the higher echelons in the work hierarchy, such as scribes, managers, or guards. It is probable that the kitchens and bakeries were intended to be communal.

The walls of the units were made of stone rubble, with two separate types of mud plaster over them. The interior walls of the rooms were plastered white. Plaster fragments were found with the remains of red, grey, or black paint on them, which seem to have come from narrow bands of red, black, and white paint around the lower portions of the walls. This style of decoration has been found at the Dakhleh Oasis site of Ayn Asil, in the governor's palace, with bands of color around the walls near the floor and at the junction with the ceiling. The walls of the habitation rooms in the governor's palace were also colored, with yellow, red, or blue. The floors of Menkaure's town site rooms were laid with a deposit of gravel that was then covered over with a layer of compacted mud, as were those at Ayn Asil. This is similar to the lane in the southernmost complex between the so-called galleries of workshops, and seems to be the conventional flooring in Old Kingdom Egyptian nonroyal buildings.

Other Pyramid Towns

Other Old Kingdom settlement sites, particularly Ein el-Gezareen in Dakhleh Oasis in the western desert and Kom el-Hisn in the northwestern Delta show the same style of construction, with apparently communal buildings and living quarters. One of the most important differences, however, in terms of the use of the separate sites, is the evidence of town-planning in the pyramid towns and the distinct lack thereof in the other sites not connected with pyramids. Ein el-Gezareen is surrounded with a thick enclosure wall, thought by the excavator to have been a defensive wall intended to keep out desert invaders of some sort, outside of which construction began when the danger was deemed gone. The town appears to have been closely connected administratively with another town in the oasis, Ayn Asil, the governorate of the oasis during the Old Kingdom;

however, despite the defensive wall and the evidence showing that rather than a self-contained habitation, it was part of a larger governmental and administrative area, the town shows no indications of having been planned. The growth of Ein el-Gezareen was organic and adapted to the space within the wall, and once building began outside the wall, the same type of growth is clear in the remains. Signs of organic urban growth, as opposed to town-planning, are likewise evident at Kom el-Hisn. This difference in urban social and architectural structure seems to be rooted in the presence of royalty and the overwhelming bureaucracy that accompanied that presence. The pyramid towns were constructed for a purpose, and in line with that purpose, were likely built each in one fell swoop, in massive construction projects to accompany the beginning of the pyramid building.

Pyramid Town Life

The lives the Egyptians within the pyramid towns were similar to those lived by Egyptians in other Old Kingdom towns. The communality of existence seems to have been one of the common reference points, with bakeries large enough to contain up to twelve ovens (in the case of Menkaure's pyramid town), and other food-processing areas that have to do with the preparation of bread, such as winnowing and grinding grain, or fish processing, as in the southernmost habitation area at Giza. The Old Kingdom towns in the Dakhleh Oasis in the Western Desert, west of modern-day Luxor, Ayn Asil and Ein el Gezareen, both show the same kind of social structure, with what appear to be communal bakeries. The habitation areas of Ayn Asil, which has been under excavation by the French for more than a decade, include a very large residence, likely the seat of the local governor. This has been particularly well-studied, and among other discoveries, the presence of quite large areas for baking and other food preparation has been noted.

The size of these areas seems to indicate a very substantial household, including members of the governor's family as well as servants and, quite possibly, administrative workers attached to the governor. This palace appears to have been in use for a succession of five governors, or about 80 years, and it is probable that in times of famine, the governor was responsible for keeping the people of the oasis fed. The presence of this type of collective food processing in a variety of Old Kingdom settlements indicates that it was likely the general method of food distribution; however, how the ingredients for bread-making were gathered, and what sort of payment was demanded for baking the bread is unknown. It appears, from the evidence at Giza, that the same kinds of communal productions were also undertaken with cloth-making and weaving.

The towns were administered by governors of one sort or another (see Document 8); textual evidence indicates that the governors of the pyramid towns were lesser sons of the king during the Fourth Dynasty, when the towns were reasonably small and compact. Later, during the Fifth Dynasty, when the towns expanded greatly in size and population, the chiefs of the towns' administration were simply governors apparently appointed by the king but with no blood attachment to the throne. The evidence from other, later pyramid towns, such as the Twelfth Dynasty town of Lahun near the Fayuum Oasis, indicate that from the governors down, the administration was profoundly hierarchical, with a well-entrenched bureaucracy that undoubtedly was a model of that of the Old Kingdom.

It seems likely, based primarily on a lack of evidence, that the manual laborers were housed elsewhere than the environs of the pyramid towns. Without the presence of either a cemetery or a substantially larger town site, it can't even be said with certainty how many workers there were, much less where and how they lived. The middle level of workers, the artisans, overseers, and scribes, have left such evidence, in the form of two cemeteries to the west of the southern complex at Giza, abutting the outcrop of the plateau. The first cemetery, closest to the complex, was one in which the overseers were buried. The second cemetery, devoted to the artisans, was connected to the first by a ramp, approximately 80 feet long. These cemeteries are fascinating because they provide evidence for the presence or absence of certain funerary protocols. The tombs of the overseers often have superstructures that are miniature pyramids made of mudbrick, which indicates that the pyramidal shape was not the right of the royal family's tombs solely. In one case, the superstructure is in the shape of a dome; made of mudbrick, it is hollow in the center with holes left for the soul to depart and reenter.

After the completion of the pyramids, the towns became geared toward the performance of the cultic rituals in the mortuary temples, in particular (see Documents 5 and 7). This meant a change in the use of the bureaucracy already in place. Whether the inhabitants of the towns were required to vacate the premises once the construction work was finished and the religious work began is unknown.

The Cemetery Fields Surrounding the Pyramids

Finally, a word needs to be said concerning the cemetery fields surrounding or near the pyramids. Some of the most important men in the Egyptian court were buried in mastabas that surrounded the pyramids' enclosure walls, although there is quite a large section of the Western Cemetery at Giza, just to the west of the Great Pyramid, which appears to have been the prerogative of the *khentiu-shay*, or palace attendants. Several of the mastabas in the Western Cemetery in particular are very large.

The titles that accompany these Giza mastabas reveal that the owners were very often men who were intimately involved in the running of the pyramid towns. They were generally royal acquaintances and so connected with the throne, even if on a very minor level. Their work titles usually began with the term "overseer," and what follows that term often indicates that the tomb owners were at one time very important people in the palace and the governmental hierarchy. A Fifth Dynasty man named Khafkhufu was the "overseer of the western cemeteries," the necropolis into which he was eventually entombed. This man was also a "king's son of his body," meaning that he was one of the king's biological sons. Another man, Tjetu, who lived during the later Sixth Dynasty, was the "overseer of the pyramid town of Akhet-Khufu," Khufu's pyramid town, and he was also the "supervisor of the *wab*-priests of Akhet-Khufu," as well as being the "overseer of the palace attendants."

What is of particular interest here is that these Egyptians, together with many others in the Giza cemeteries, chose to be buried close to their work. This makes it likely that they also lived in the area, and perhaps even within one of the pyramid towns themselves. Their families, including wives and children, were very often mentioned in the reliefs, as were dependents, such as men who oversaw the tomb owners' fields and works, and women who nursed their children. The hierarchical system of the government worked on every level of Egyptian society, from the broadest, on a national stage, to the smallest, the family.

THE WORKERS

The use of the corvée system allowed the Egyptians to manage effectively the manpower they were able to command, separating workers into gangs, working them for only a few months at a time. This ensured fresh working crews at the end of the work period, ready to take over, without having exhausted the outgoing workers to the point of death.

A considerable amount of material gives insight into the work gangs of the pyramids, the Giza Plateau pyramids in particular, and other monumental buildings of the Old Kingdom. The workers were well-organized and the work hierarchical. Despite the general paucity of evidence, enough has been gleaned to give a fairly full idea of how the work was divided. There was a tripartite composition of labor: crews or gangs, phyles or units, and "divisions." The crews were divided into two groups, and each of them was divided into four, and later five, phyles or units, which were further split into two or more divisions, each of which had possibly ten men. The rotation seemed to be based on a 10-month schedule, with phyles and divisions replacing each other at irregular intervals. Thus, the work was continuous with fresh workers at staggered periods that ensured that the work was ongoing with as few major interruptions as possible.

Names were given to each of the various gangs, phyles, and divisions; the names of the phyles, in particular, lasted from Dynasty One to Dynasty Six and the end of the Old Kingdom—*wer* (The Great Ones), *setj* (The Scatterers?), *wadjet* (The Hale Ones), and *nedjes* (The Poor Ones). What is of particular interest about these names, which were only used during the Old Kingdom, is their apparent origin as, or strong similarity to, naval terms. This is true of many Old Kingdom titles, most of which have been found inscribed on rocks at quarries and mine sites in the Eastern and Western Deserts far from the river or the Red or Mediterranean Seas. The use of naval titles for officers having no connection with the river is a clear indication of the importance of the Nile and water transportation from the earliest periods of Egyptian history. It appears that these terms were so entrenched in Egyptian working society that they became all-purpose working terms that were no longer indicative of specific duties, but rather of hierarchical position.

The earliest evidence for phyles comes from the reign of Den, during the First Dynasty. These phyles, along with others from the First Dynasty, appear to have been used at the royal court, rather than for state-building projects. Phyles during the Second and Third Dynasties are linked with servant duties in the court, religious proceedings, cultic rituals, and more mundane tasks in the temples. The first evidence for phyles used as work gangs on the pyramids is from the reign of Sneferu, the first king of Dynasty Four. Previous to this, all evidence for phyles came from inscriptions left on ephemeral artifacts, such as pottery, and plates that seemed to serve as some sort of docket. During the Fourth Dynasty, however, all the inscriptions are found on monumental architecture, a shift that may indicate the introduction of a new use for the phyle system, for work on the funerary architecture projects instigated by the king.

The graffiti left by these gangs of workmen indicate that they were of two types; those associated with the construction of the pyramids and those associated with the later cultic activity. Some of the evidence for phyles has been found on private funerary monuments, in particular on the mastaba tombs to the west of Khufu's pyramid, and is only associated with the priestly or cultic phyles. The owners of the mastabas on which the graffiti was discovered were close to the throne, many of them serving as viziers, a position second only to the king, and were undoubtedly given permission by the king to make use of the system. Additional graffiti on the Giza Plateau indicates that at least one tomb owner was granted permission by the king to second two phyles to help in the construction of his mastaba. These phyles were sent from a crew, and were not accompanied by the other two phyles. Several Old Kingdom inscriptions indicate that this type of building at the king's expense was not uncommon.

WOMEN IN THE OLD KINGDOM

The work of building the pyramids was that of men, or so we assume. Generally, women were left out of the historical record that dealt with the specifics of hard labor. According to tomb reliefs, women's work involved household tasks for most of Egyptian history. There is an exception to this and that is found in the evidence for the role of women during the Old Kingdom. The Old Kingdom seems to have been a period of "settling in" with regard to nearly every facet of the culture, a period in which later entrenched societal elements are first being tested and either accepted or rejected. This applies to the role of women, as well as to religious doctrine, societal mores, and governmental bureaucracy, among others, and the textual record, mainly in the form of titles, indicates that during the Old Kingdom, women held much higher positions in society and the government than at any other period. The types of titles held by women during this period indicate that they held positions of relative power; it is the only period during which women hold religious titles, including those of priestesses and overseers of priestesses, for example.

Generally, women were priestesses for female deities, although some exceptions have been found to this. Hathor and Neith were the deities most represented by female priestesses; it appears that the women who had these titles were either musicians or official mourners, rather than performers of the cults associated with the goddesses. This is not to say that their roles in the temples were not important. On the contrary, they were integral to the functioning of the daily rites and ceremonies. In the cult of Hathor, women were assigned the role of divine *meret*-singers of Upper and Lower Egypt, the exact function of which is unknown. The cult of Neith used women in the capacity of official lamenters, known as *djeret*-mourners. The *djeret*-mourners impersonated two goddesses, Isis and Nephthys. In mythology, in the shape of kites (a hawk-like bird), these goddesses hunted for the corpse of Osiris, killed by his brother, Seth. When they found him, they wheeled over his body in the sky, screeching their sorrow. While the mourners' exact duties are, again, unknown, official lamenters are portrayed on later tomb reliefs, dressed in costumes of white robes, wailing, waving their hands in the air, and often, throwing dirt on their heads.

Women in the Old Kingdom also filled positions of administration, such as overseers of not only priestesses, as mentioned above, but also overseers of doctors and palace attendants, or *khenty-shay*. It seems that women were generally overseers of women, and men of men. While female doctors are not attested in the records, it is assumed that a female overseer of doctors would have been responsible for female doctors, and thus, the practice of medicine has been added to the list of occupations for women that did not survive the Old Kingdom. Other administrative positions held by women included overseers of midwives, dancers, weavers, and food supplies.

Women are depicted in the tomb reliefs of the period as participating in the world outside the house boundaries to a greater extent than in later periods. Certain tasks are clearly divided along gender lines, but women and men are more often shown working together and spending recreational time together, indicating less confined and secluded lives in general. Women are shown overseeing household activities such as the capturing of fowl, and performing such duties as working on boats. In one scene of war, a woman is shown stabbing a raider while another woman assists a man and boy in breaking a foreigner's bow. While such scenes may depict incidents that were anomalous in Egyptian life of the Old Kingdom, the fact of their absence from equally bellicose scenes in the Middle and New Kingdoms may point to a different attitude toward the place of women in war and perhaps in society generally.

Building the pyramids was a task that took laborers from all levels of Egyptian society, from the king and his architects and engineers down to the men hewing the stone blocks. The undertaking, therefore, was one that could have been said to be the work of the entire country. On a national level, without the rigid hierarchical bureaucracy that existed throughout Egypt that afforded the government with census information, and without the complete power the king wielded over his subjects, the building of the pyramids would not have been possible. They were the culmination of the labor of all levels of society, of most of the departments in the Egyptian bureaucracy, and overarching royal control.

CHAPTER 6

THE ARCHITECTURE AND ART OF THE PYRAMID COMPLEX

ARCHITECTURE

Very few of the valley temples are extant; most of them either lie under cultivation or have been completely robbed of their limestone blocks. The few that remain are Khufu's, Khafre's, and Menkaure's at Giza; Sahure's and Neferirkare's (subsequently usurped by Niuserre) at Abusir; Unas' and Pepi II's at South Saqqara. The other valley temples were either destroyed for their precut blocks of stone or have yet to be discovered. Those that remain undiscovered are likely lying beneath cultivation or habitation, and are thus almost permanently unavailable. Khufu's valley temple was only discovered as a result of a canal project; during excavation of a swathe of land between two roads that run beside the Giza plateau, the backhoes encountered a number of large, finished limestone blocks with the cartouche of Khufu inscribed on them. This find has provided the only indication of the situation of Khufu's valley temple, but as a result of the canal, the roads, and the surrounding habitation, further excavation is impossible.

The valley temples that remain, however, indicate that similar programs of architecture and relief were used in these structures throughout the pyramid complexes of the Old Kingdom. As no valley temple remains completely intact, it is necessary to compare the remains of all temples to come up with as complete a program of relief as possible. The canal entrance and ramp were to be the metaphorical entrance of the king into the afterlife, and were intended to serve as the beginning of the king's afterlife tour through Egypt. The purposes for this were both prosaic, in the gathering of provisions, and less so, in the overseeing of the continued ruling of the country. The reliefs that depict the gathering of provisions consist of food and other stuffs being brought to the king by bearers, both foreign and Egyptian. The ruling of the country, on the other hand, was illustrated by reliefs of the king as a sphinx, trampling and slaying his enemies. Thus, the king was shown in both active and passive royal duty.

Within the temple itself, in the store rooms or antechambers, the king is represented either walking into the temple and toward the pyramid, or walking away from the pyramid, and out of the complex. The notion of movement is important to the perception of the king's ongoing interest in Egypt and his rule. Although his body is dead, his various spirits continue to work for the benefit of the country from the afterlife and in concert with the king on the mundane throne. Part of this idea of movement and cooperative rule from beyond the grave is shown in the reliefs through the medium of the king offering to the gods, on his own behalf and on behalf of Egypt.

The Position of the Art in the Architecture

In general, the architecture of the valley temples was similar, although likely not exactly the same for each temple. Usually, one ramp or slipway led from the water to the temple, although in the case of Sahure's temple, two ramps lead from the canal or river, one from the east and one from the south. The primary ramp seems to have been the eastern one, and it seems likely that, given the metaphorically charged nature of the west as the abode of the dead, this ramp was the one against which the great funerary barque of the king moored when the time came. This area of transition between the Nile Valley and the desert served as a metaphor for the king's entrance into the afterworld, a place of movement from life into death. The southern ramp into Sahure's temple was probably the ramp used for temple provisions, and initially, for the cargo boats. While most of the limestone for the interior blocks of the pyramids came from quarries on the west bank in the near vicinity of the construction site, the more exotic stones such as basalt and granite, were brought downriver from the Fayuum and even Aswan. This meant that mooring sites for the cargo boats were important from almost the beginning of the building process, and therefore, it is probable that the ramps were among the first completed structures in the complexes.

The entrance to the temple proper was through a portico, or columned hall, that served as a foyer. In Sahure's temple, this area was paved in black basalt with columns of pink granite, shaped to resemble date palms. The ceiling of the portico was constructed of massive blocks of granite, the underside of which had a relief of yellow stars on a blue ground. The main building of Sahure's valley temple consisted of a single room, the walls and columns of which were decorated with reliefs. For the most part, the reliefs have been destroyed but enough remains to show the king offering to deities in their shrines, the king as a sphinx trampling his enemies, the royal funeral barque, and the king suckling at the breast of an unknown goddess, a scene that includes the goddess, Nekhbet, and the god, Khnum. Nekhbet was one of the goddesses associated with the royal crown, and was usually depicted as a vulture, or as a woman with a vulture headdress. Khnum, a ram-headed deity, was a creator god, and his presence, together with Nekhbet's, may be as reinforcement for the king's entrance into the afterlife. Other relief fragments depict marsh scenes, offering-bearers, and scenes of animal butchery.

The causeways that lead from the valley temples to the pyramid temples and pyramids were simply walled and covered walkways that ran from the valley temple to the mortuary complex and pyramid. The finest remaining example of this is Unas' causeway, and most of the pavement survives along with some scattered sections of walls. It was originally 2,460 feet long, making it one of the longest. It was roofed with great blocks of limestone, with a gap left between them to let in light. Other causeways were completely roofed in, some had clerestory lighting near the top, and, in the beginning, they were unroofed. The causeways that were completely roofed in must have had lamps at regular intervals, primarily to light the way, but also to make the reliefwork on the walls' interiors visible. Initially, the causeways were meant to keep the body of the dead king hidden during the funerary procession, but after this had occurred, they were presumably used to keep the rituals associated with the valley and mortuary temples secret. Enough remains of the various causeways to indicate that there were doors at the upper end, near the pyramid's enclosure wall, likely to facilitate the movement of people. Without them, the only entrance to the mortuary temple would have been through the valley temple, half a mile away.

The causeways led to the mortuary temple, the area reserved for the worshipping the cult of the dead king (see Document 4). This was a much larger building than the valley temple, built as a rectangle with the longest sides facing east and west. It was comprised of five separate components: an entrance much like the one in the valley temples with columns, a courtyard surrounded by columns that appeared to have been used for sacrificing animals for the royal cult and offerings, a room with statue niches that had once contained statues of the king and other deities, a hall for offerings, and finally, numbers of storerooms. The mortuary temple was used on a daily basis by the priests responsible for the upkeep and maintenance of the royal cult. This involved sacrificing animals for the daily offerings, presenting those offerings, and generally ensuring the dead king was provisioned with everything he might need day by day. As such, it was built on a much grander scale than the valley temples, and was the focal point of the complex after the king's death.

The materials used in the construction of the mortuary temples (also known as the pyramid or upper temples) were of the finest quality, reflecting both the importance of the king and of his cultic establishment. The primary stone used for building the temples was limestone; however, more expensive stones, often quarried and brought from great distances, were used for the finer touches. Red and black granite from Aswan was used for columns and flooring, respectively, and was also used irrespective of color for doorways. Alabaster, probably quarried from sites along the west bank of the river, in the area around modern-day Cairo, was used both for flooring and for wall paneling. Basalt was used for flooring and was likely quarried in the Fayum. The expense in manpower and haulage of these precious materials, made precious by that very expense, must have been huge, but the end product would have been the finest construction of the time.

The entranceway was a rectangular columned hall. The Egyptians called it the "house of the great," and it seems to have been a gathering place for dignitaries on the day of the funeral. The entrance led through a doorway into a covered corridor that itself lead to an open courtyard, which was surrounded by a columned walkway, topped with limestone slabs that were decorated with carved stars painted yellow on a blue background, as in the valley temple. Each of the columns was carved on the surface facing into the courtyard with the names of kings. The corridor between the entrance hall and the open courtyard was decorated with reliefs on both the inner and outer sides. The walls of this corridor were decorated with scenes of the king's life, such as fishing, hunting, singing, dancing, and the departure and arrival of a sea-going expedition.

The five niches in the statue room were, at one time, filled with statues of either the king or gods. None of these statues remain; however, literary evidence from a cache of papyrus found in the mortuary temple of Neferirkare, an otherwise little-known Fifth Dynasty king, indicates that among the statues were a representation of the king wearing the crown of Upper Egypt, a second of him wearing the crown of Lower Egypt, and a third statue was of Osiris. The identities of the other two statues are not mentioned in the text, but they were undoubtedly associated with both the passage of the king through the afterlife and his eventual abode therein.

The Architecture of the Tombs Surrounding the Giza Pyramids

The tombs of the noblemen and their families, and of the palace retainers that surrounded the pyramids at the various pyramid fields were of several types, delineated by George Reisner, an American Egyptologist of the early twentieth century. It appears from the titles and epithets used that the style of tomb greatly depended on the wealth of the owner, even more than that owner's level in the palace hierarchy. Thus, the more wealth an owner had, the larger and more architecturally complicated his tomb was. It would seem logical that the higher the standard of artistic expression, the more wealth displayed by the owner; however, this is not always the case. Some of the smaller mastabas have finer reliefs than do the larger ones. An example of this is the mastaba of Neferbauptah in the Western Cemetery, which is smaller than the others in the same familial complex, but which has the finest reliefwork. It may well be that such owners were more concerned with architectural size, something that could be seen from the outside, rather than a high quality of artistic workmanship, but that is something that will remain unknown.

The tombs were built with casings of the local nummulitic limestone, or limestone that was particularly full of fossils, something that could cause difficulties for the artists carving the reliefs. Within the casings, a variety of different material was thrown as fill. Sometimes, large numbers of pots were used as fill, gently enough placed within the limestone walls that they were not broken. Vast quantities of limestone chips were also used as fill, as were accumulations of rubble that consisted of smaller and larger stones and sediment. Pieces of broken and chipped granite have also been found, which has posed something of a mystery, as no granite is found in the surrounding tombs. It seems likely that the granite from older mastabas' statues or offering tables was used, perhaps already broken, perhaps broken to size. This is an indication of the longevity, or lack thereof, of the upkeep of the tombs, as it would only be possible to scavenge from tombs that had stopped being looked after and used.

The mastabas are almost uniformly destroyed down to a few courses of rock, although some remain in remarkably good condition. It is unfortunate that the largest mastaba in the Western Cemetery, given the appellation G 2000, is anonymous, as it is also one of the most complete. Generally, however, all that remains are anywhere from five to seven courses of stone. While this is not helpful in studying the art, it is particularly helpful in studying the architecture of the mastabas, giving very clear indications of how the mastabas were built, the materials used, and how the various features, such as serdab and tomb shafts, were incorporated into the whole.

The tomb shafts were generally dug into the core of the mastabas. Sometimes the accompanying tomb's walls were shored up with limestone but more often not, so the tombs were simply excavated holes in the mastabas, dug as occasion and need arose. The serdabs, on the other hand, were built into the tomb walls, close to the offering or false door stelae, and usually directly over the primary tomb. It was often the case, however, that with the less wealthy tomb owners' mastabas, the "streets" between the mastabas were taken over and used as serdabs. This was accomplished by blocking off the area between two mastabas with limestone blocks and incorporating the foreign mastaba's wall into the serdab. A similar procedure was used for creating offering areas.

The streets and avenues between the mastabas was a method also used by those who couldn't afford even the smallest, simplest mastaba. This was often done on the plateau, where space was at a premium and spiritual value of the highest. As many as three burials could be placed between small mastabas, and many more between larger ones. These were the simplest of graves, two sides of which were the opposite sides of two mastabas. They were jerry-built and completely undecorated, with two odd exceptions. During one season of excavation in the Western Cemetery, three of these intrusive tombs were discovered along one street. Each of the tombs had an offering place, usually carved very crudely out of limestone, used either in the roof or in the two constructed walls, and each of the tombs had a reused (that is, stolen from another mastaba) offering stela used in the construction of the walls. The stelae were placed with the unused backs facing into the tomb chamber itself. Whether these were simply coincidences is unknown, as the chance to excavate such tombs is now a relatively rare event; however, it seems likely that the offering bowls (for lack of a better term) and stelae were used deliberately. The placement of the stelae with the worked side facing into the fill, rather than the tomb, was so done perhaps to make use of the spiritual nature of the stone, coupled with a reluctance to put someone else's name in one's tomb. On a more prosaic note, it could simply have been that these stelae were convenient, large blocks of already-worked stone, which meant less work for the tomb's constructors.

ART

To most uninformed observers, Egyptian art is much of a muchness; in other words, it looks the same no matter what period you choose. The decoration in Old Kingdom tombs appears to be identical to that in the tombs of the New Kingdom, and without the help of dated inscriptions, it is not always possible for art historians to date paintings or objects securely to one period or another. The portrayal of the human figure changed little throughout the history, and certain peculiarities of style remained constant, including difficulties with proportion that were never entirely overcome. The methods of drawing the reliefs to an artistic "canon of proportions"[1] that conformed to a squared grid was used from the Old Kingdom to the Late Period, and in the most general of terms, most ancient Egyptian art is recognizable as Egyptian.

Although there are apparent similarities in Egyptian art from one period to the next, the similarities end with the superficial glance, and very real and distinct differences in style and content emerge. The art from the Old Kingdom and earlier is some of the most beautiful, and the most skillfully rendered in Egyptian history. It does not come from commoners' tombs, however, but from royal complexes, highly placed noblemen's tombs, and the tombs of palace workers, and overseers of workmen on the Giza plateau, and mayors of Elephantine in the far south, among others. Everyone, therefore, who had a tomb that was well-built enough to last, was someone who had a connection of some sort with the palace, and therefore, was able to requisition the royal craftsmen and workmen in the construction and decoration of their tombs. This, of course, meant that the work done on the tombs was, quite literally, work fit for a king, of the highest quality. It is important to keep in mind that we are forming an opinion of a body of work that is skewed by the lack of comparison of work from lesser workmen. Despite this shortage, however, or perhaps because of it, the art of the Old Kingdom stands as particularly beautiful examples in the Egyptian canon.

Old Kingdom art seems to have been almost exclusively limited to funerary contexts. This situation is likely the result of the vagaries of preservation. In comparison with later periods, very little of anything remains from the Old Kingdom; however, it is possible that the makers of what we now consider to be art were the possession of the king, to be doled out by him as favors from the crown. Wood, plaster, and stone surfaces were painted with vibrant colors in tombs and royal funerary complexes. There are remarkable reliefs on the walls of the tombs of very wealthy Egyptians. They portray the owner of the tomb and wife and family enjoying the leisure pursuits they enjoyed in life, boating, duck-hunting, fishing, entertaining, listening to music, eating, to name a few. The tomb owner is always shown as the owner of a large estate with plenty of peasants to work the land and provide for the household. The Twelfth Dynasty in the Middle Kingdom was a period that has left a large number of tomb models of fishermen, the biannual cattle count, granaries, butcheries, a cow giving birth with the help of two men, and a wide range of other activities. Time and the weather have removed most of the color from the reliefs, although it is still possible to find some outstanding and vivid examples. The geese from a Fourth Dynasty tomb at Meidum belonging to Itet are a stellar example. The six geese are positioned on a ground-line, and are painted with an exactness of style that allows for the species to be identified. Each feather is painted separately, and the result is a bucolic scene of remarkable realism.

The style used by the Egyptian artists did not change and appears to have developed very quickly in the Early Dynasty period, and with the advent of the Third Dynasty, the artistic canon seems fully realized. From examinations of what remains of the generally destroyed pyramid complexes, the programs of temple and causeway relief are remarkably similar over a period of hundreds of years. This indicates that not only was the program set, but that adherence to the specific agenda of the reliefs was important. The Egyptians did not appear to have created art for its own sake; the very concept of "art" seems to have been an unknown.

Therefore, the reliefs, statues, and other decorations were meant to fulfill a purpose.

One of the enduring questions regarding the use of the pyramid complexes has centered on the reliefwork and the direction in which it was intended to be read. Was the program of relief intended to be applicable to the priests and the funerary procession as it went into the pyramid, or was it intended for the use of the dead king, as he made his way out of the complex and into the afterlife in the sky? The same question has been posed regarding the Pyramid Texts, and in neither case can answers be made definitively. What is certain, however, is the use to which the reliefs were put and the fact that generally (although not specifically) the Pyramid Texts and the reliefs in the temples and causeway were intended for use in an ongoing ritual sense. The temple reliefs appear to have been suited to the particular rituals to be enacted within each temple, and those in the causeway seem to indicate, in a few representative and commonly used scenes, the nature of the king's role on earth, a role that would be identical in the afterlife.

Artistic Style

The types of reliefwork that were used to decorate the walls were generally either religious or mundane. The religious reliefs were those intended to help the tomb owner into the afterlife, while the mundane reliefs were what the tomb owner's life had been like while he or she was alive and what they hoped it would be like in the afterlife. From this, we have some idea of the lives led by the wealthiest Egyptians. The art in the pyramid complexes was no different from that in nonroyal Egyptians' tombs in basic content, but the scope was poles apart. During the king's lifetime, the land of Egypt, with its inhabitants, its climate, its foreign acquisitions, its religious life, its judicial life, was all the responsibility of the king. For all intents and purposes, he was Egypt. This was more than simply a moral obligation to do the best that was possible for the land and the people; the king was part of the mythological landscape of Egypt, and as such, he was the very soil the farmers used and the water in the river and the sun in the sky.

Even without daily offerings, the ongoing celestial presence of the king was made certain through the reliefs, painted or carved, on the interior walls of the mortuary temples, depicting lines of offering bearers carrying such goods as wine, beer, bread, fruit, vegetables, pigeons and quails in cages, and herdsmen bringing cattle, antelope, gazelles, goats, ducks, and geese. The rituals he performed in the temples, or which were performed in his name, were responsible for the movement of the sun, the coming of night and return of day, and the level of the Nile during the inundation, among many other natural occurrences. These responsibilities remained a part of the king after he died. Thus, the decoration of his mortuary temple, the building dedicated to the worship of his ongoing presence in the afterlife, had to reflect the complexity of the regal life, a complexity that was not part of the nonroyal life.

The canon of Egyptian art of the Old Kingdom is relatively narrow in the schemes used. It has been broken down into three main types: a single figure, a row of single figures, and grouped figures. These were organized in registers, or bands of decoration, each with their own ground-line. It is tempting to think that one is meant to "read" the registers as an open view, with the groups in the registers all on the same piece of ground over a wide area; however, this is not the case. Often, a series of registers are overseen by a single larger figure of the king or deity, and it seems that, rather than occurring simultaneously, the registers are meant to express discrete actions, not necessarily in the same place or at the same time.

A single figure, in a royal context, was either the king or a deity. This figure was always the largest in a room's or corridor's reliefs; the other figures were generally at least half the size of the king or deity. This had the effect of both drawing the eyes toward the king or deity, and making very clear the relative importance of the large and smaller figures. The larger figure was generally sited to one end of the registers, and nearly always placed facing out of the temples, to receive the incoming offerings or prisoners or worshippers. Portraying this figure, royal or divine, facing outward from the temples, was intended to place the king or deity firmly within the temple, as a type of abode after death. It also worked as did the sizes of the figures, to emphasize the fact that the figure was one toward which life moved, rather than one that moved toward anything.

Lines of single figures were used to convey movement, as in processions of people bringing offerings or other goods, or as processions of prisoners. Often, those lines could be followed from one room to another, indicating the passage of the processions through the temples, thus movement through space. These were often shown at close to ground level, and while important to the overall scheme of decoration, might have been considered to be background action to the primary scenes at eye level or higher. Thus, long lines of women facing into the temple and representing, for example, the various estates of the king, would be depicted bearing offerings of various kinds. The offerings were of great consequence to the deceased king and the ongoing rituals enacted for his cult, but they were not of particular mythological or symbolic value otherwise.

Groups of people or animals were often used to indicate action of some kind. The hunting, birding, and fishing scenes are good cases in point. The figures of animals, fowl, and fish are shown overlapping each other, sometimes looking over their shoulders rather than looking straight ahead, and are shown in a confused state. While these types of scenes show the daily activities of the king, they also fulfill a less obvious purpose, that of portraying chaos. From the very beginning of Egyptian history, the bringing together of the two lands was seen metaphorically as a triumph of order against chaos. This can be seen in the sporting tableaux, where the chaotic movement of the fauna is offset by the surrounding human figures representing order. The movement here is through time, and intended to convey a single action. Should more than one action be necessary to communicate an event, the groups were put one above the other, the earliest on top.

The content of the Old Kingdom reliefs has provided anomalous examples of certain scenes, one of the most famous of which is the depiction of starving Bedouin from the causeway reliefs of Unas at South Saqqara, and elsewhere. They are limited to the Old Kingdom, and there is some discussion whether they portray the effects of a specific famine, or whether they are meant to be more generally understood as a representation of particularly difficult climatic conditions within the reign of Unas. It seems most likely that they are meant to indicate that famine occurred during the reign of Unas, rather than referring to a specific episode. These types of generalized scenes occur throughout nearly all periods of Egyptian history, particularly in the tombs of high court officials of the New Kingdom, but it is only in the Old Kingdom that they are found in specifically royal art.

The remains of Unas' causeway show that there was a wide variety of painted reliefwork, both mythological and worldly, and that the program of relief was structured to align with the uses of the valley and mortuary temples. At the lower end of the causeway, near the valley, the decoration was primarily mythological in content, with the intention of protecting the king during the funerary procession when he was potentially vulnerable, and likely also for this reason, all the figures faced toward the valley temple. This included reliefs of captive foreign prisoners being lead by deities to the king, indicating the king's supremacy over foreign lands, and, similarly to the valley temple reliefs, the king as sphinx trampling enemies. The king, no longer able to protect either himself or the country, was reliant on the deities to perform that service for him in the afterlife.

The upper causeway was dedicated to provisioning the king in the afterlife and depicted scenes of the finishing touches being put to the pyramids, such as moving the capstone, or pyramidion, into place. In the causeway of Sahure at Abusir, these were arranged in five registers, and also included scenes of dancers, wrestlers, archers in competition, processions of soldiers, the preparation of offerings, and starving foreigners, presumed to be Bedouin, sitting as captives. This final image is the one also found in Unas' causeway, and is one of the most famous of all the reliefs from the various causeways. The figures in these scenes all face toward the mortuary temple, as if accompanying the king into the afterlife.

The pyramids of the Fourth Dynasty and most of the Fifth were anepigraphic; they were not decorated with any style or type of art. The chamber walls and entranceways of the pyramid of Unas, the last king of the Fifth Dynasty were covered with Pyramid Texts, and the ceilings were painted blue with yellow stars. The pyramids of the Sixth Dynasty were similarly decorated. The hieroglyphs themselves are arguably a type of art, and indeed, in some instances, they kept their intrinsic representational meaning; however their primary purpose was linguistic, rather than representational, a significant difference from the reliefwork found elsewhere in the pyramid complexes as a whole. The other buildings that made up the complexes—the pyramid or mortuary temple, the valley temple, and the causeway linking the two—were elaborately decorated with reliefwork on the walls and with statuary in niches along the temple walls. This decoration was representational and symbolic, intended to present the world of the king both in this life and in the afterlife, and as such had powerful spiritual meaning for the Egyptians.

The Artwork in the Tombs Surrounding the Giza Pyramids

The tombs surrounding the Giza plateau are often filled with reliefwork that shows portions of Old Kingdom society and culture at work. It is abundant enough and in enough varying states of completion that it is possible to follow the ancient steps taken to decorate the walls, something that would otherwise be lost. Either full painted reliefwork was used or simply paint over plaster. The latter option seemed to be the less expensive one. The relief option took longer, required more skilled craftsmen, including sculptors, and would have been more costly in terms of time and labor, hence more costly financially.

Because the walls were generally made from nummulitic limestone, which is a stone with many hard fossil inclusions, it was first necessary to create a smooth surface on the stone, and this was done by plastering the face that was to be decorated with a pinkish-colored plaster. The idea was to even out the bumps in the stone and to make it easier to carve, which meant that over relatively smooth parts of the stone, the plaster was only a tenth of an inch deep and over dips and spaces in the stone face, the plaster could be as much as a third of an inch. Once the surface had been prepared, the images were drawn with red ink. These were corrected and gone over by a master craftsman in black ink.

The next step was to cut into the inked lines with a chisel that had a tip that was less than a tenth of an inch wide. Once this was done, then the background was chipped away with a tool that had a slightly scalloped edge that was about a fifth of an inch wide. After the removal of the background, the relief images stood approximately one twentieth of an inch deep. The figures were smoothed and their edges rounded with abrasive, probably fine sand, and then they were painted. The paint still remains in those tombs that were carved in relief and then painted. This seemed to be the more expensive option, however, as often, the reliefs were just painted onto a plastered surface, and the paint has either faded or been chipped away along with the plaster, leaving archaeologists no clue as to the name or rank of the tomb's owner and its inhabitants.

The subject matter of the reliefs in these tombs was considerably less rarefied than that of the royals'. While the tomb owners were often shown in front of lines of men and women bearing offerings, they were also shown watching over work in the fields, often accompanied by their overseers. They were, sometimes, overseers themselves, and were shown beside their superiors, or were shown as an adjunct to the larger house. This style of prosaic representation was one that was used throughout Egypt's history, wherever decorated tombs were built or dug out of the rock. It was a style that was never used by royalty, likely for a number of reasons, one of which must have been the place of the king in the afterlife as ruler of the country and shepherd of its people.

CONCLUSION

Each of the various facets of the pyramid complex was as integral as the next for the afterlife of the king. The pyramids themselves would have been useless to the dead king, without the rituals that were performed on a daily basis on his behalf in the mortuary temple; the art in the mortuary temple was vital for the rituals to work and the illustrations of the deities and the king in the afterlife enforced the desired result of those rituals. The valley temple was built primarily for the arrival of the dead king on the day of his burial, and the causeway leading to the main complex from the valley temple provided the necessary secrecy from the eyes of commoners; the art in both of these buildings was intended to aid in the proper process of burial, and to ensure the beginning of the king's afterlife voyage was done in accordance with what the deities required. Each portion of the reliefs was created to fulfill a purpose.

It is impossible to separate the spiritual and metaphoric from the mundane and simple, when looking at Egyptian art and architecture, as with so much else in ancient Egypt. Without doubt, the common Egyptians lived lives that were relatively ordinary, likely concerned primarily with food and shelter, and not as concerned with the less mundane aspects of life. The king, however, was the person who was responsible for maintaining the life of the country, as well as the lives of his people. His life and title seem to have operated in both the spiritual and the mundane worlds, a necessity for the good of Egypt as a whole. The pyramids with their vast complexes were part of that, keeping Egypt in order from the otherworld.

NOTE

1. Gay Robins, *Proportion and Style in Ancient Egyptian Art*. Austin: University of Texas Press, 1994, passim.

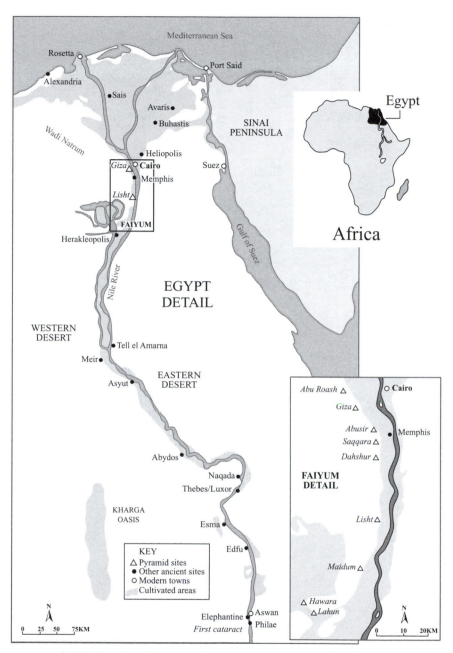

A map of Old Kingdom Egypt, with an inset indicating the placement of the various pyramid fields discussed. © Carrie Cockburn

The most important Old Kingdom pyramids shown in section with their entrances and burial chambers.

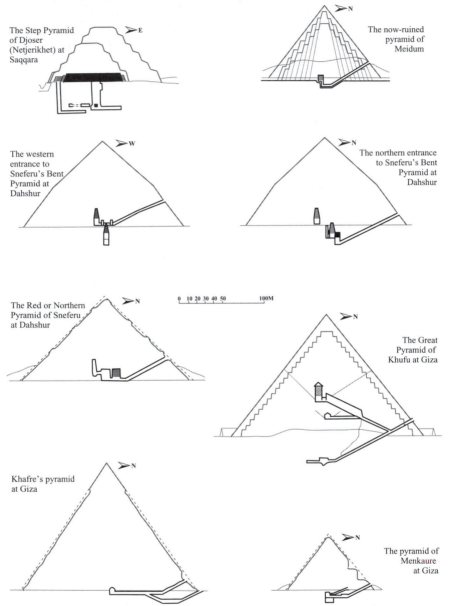

The Step Pyramid of Djoser (Netjerikhet) at Saqqara

The now-ruined pyramid of Meidum

The western entrance to Sneferu's Bent Pyramid at Dahshur

The northern entrance to Sneferu's Bent Pyramid at Dahshur

The Red or Northern Pyramid of Sneferu at Dahshur

0 10 20 30 40 50   100M

The Great Pyramid of Khufu at Giza

Khafre's pyramid at Giza

The pyramid of Menkaure at Giza

The diagram of the main pyramids in sections shows, among other things, the placement of the various tomb chambers. It is significant that the only one placed within the pyramid's body is that of Khufu. © Carrie Cockburn

Djoser's Step Pyramid. The six steps of Djoser's Step Pyramid (Dynasty Three) are visible. The great courtyard, viewed to the north from the enclosure wall, was used for ceremonies, such as the *Sed* Festival, during which the king would run around two broadly spaced markers to demonstrate his physical ability to continue ruling Egypt. © Timothy Hellum

These engaged columns are found in the main entrance to Djoser's Step Pyramid in the southeast corner of the enclosure wall. They were made in ever-decreasing drums, shaped like bundles of papyri. They remained attached to the walls, indicating, perhaps, the ancient stoneworker's still-developing and still-uncertain skills in dealing with the properties of stone. © Carrie Cockburn

These statues of Djoser, located within the enclosure wall of the Step Pyramid, are in various states of completion, allowing a glimpse into the stages of a royal statue's production. Their unfinished state may be the result of the sudden death of the king, and the immediate cessation of all his commissioned work with the ascension of the new king to the throne. © Carrie Cockburn

The Bent Pyramid has been aptly named, evidenced by the distinct turn in the sides, creating a broader platform. Much of the outer limestone casing remains, giving one of the few indications of what the pyramids must have looked like when newly constructed. © Timothy Hellum

Khufu's Sun Boat. Found in a pit beside the pyramid, the boat's wood shows signs that the boat was used at least once before it was dismantled and stored in the pit. Whether it was used to carry other dead kings' bodies to the Giza Plateau is unknown; however, it does not seem to have been used more than once, and it corresponds with the reliefs of funeral boats found in later tombs. © Timothy Hellum

The Sphinx and Khafre's Pyramid. The sphinx was carved from a natural outcropping of stone, giving the lower body its weathered appearance. Khafre's pyramid, behind the sphinx, retains its limestone covering. Metal poles have been placed in a vertical position on top of each of the pyramids, to their original height, giving a good idea of how much has been lost over the millennia. © Timothy Hellum

Menkaure's Pyramid, never finished. The blocks were cut back and finished around the original entrance, as can be seen in the lower right portion of the pyramid. Although it is also much smaller than the other two Giza pyramids, the materials and workmanship were of the same high quality as the others. © Timothy Hellum

Unas' Pyramid. Unlike other earlier pyramids, Unas' Pyramid has suffered greatly due to poor materials and construction. Seen here from the southwest, the outer casing blocks are visible. The long causeway led from the opposite side to canal or the Nile itself. © Timothy Hellum

Tomb relief of donkeys. This piece of relief, now in the Royal Ontario Museum, was originally from the tomb of Metjetji, an official in the late Fifth or early Sixth Dynasty in Saqqara. The donkeys are shown with sacks of grain tied to their backs in front of a depiction of a sheaf of wheat. The hieroglyph above the donkeys reads "the balance of sheaves: 1,300." Note that there are only nine legs for five donkeys. With permission of the Royal Ontario Museum, © ROM.

CHAPTER 7

INTERPRETATION AND LEGACY

INTRODUCTION

It is hard to overestimate the lure of ancient Egypt to modern man. Since the winding down of pharaonic Egyptian civilization and its eventual conquest by Alexander the Great in 394 B.C.E., the nearly completely buried monuments have provided travelers with the tantalizing knowledge that the remains of a once-great civilization lay beneath their feet. Before the decipherment of the Egyptian hieroglyphic writing system and language in 1822 by Jean-François Champollion, the monuments kept their secrets to themselves, the language written on them remaining pretty pictures, mute and without further Egyptian meaning. As a result, interpreters could assign any meaning they desired to them, and the notion of a mysterious Egypt grew.

The pyramids, as the largest and most visible representations of ancient Egyptian civilization, became a focus for outside interpretation. They represented a sense of timelessness, and an idea of reaching toward the heavens. They were also representative of the vast wealth of ancient Egypt, it being believed that untold treasures were buried within them. Because of their size and their apparent indestructibility, they became part of the seven wonders of the ancient world, a list that began with the ancient Greeks and was finalized during the Middle Ages. This sense of awe, compounded by the projection of what might be considered man's desire and perhaps yearning for mystery onto the pyramids, meant that Egypt as a whole was taken into the modern imagination and there it has stayed.

EGYPTOMANIA

Ancient

The influence of ancient Egypt upon later peoples began with the Egyptians themselves—a son of Rameses I (so Rameses II), Prince Khaemwaset, was particularly interested in the works of his forefathers, and set about reconstructing the monuments most in need of restoration. Those included Unas' pyramid, and he left an inscription on the pyramid to indicate his work.

In the first millennium, the Greeks displayed evidence of Egyptomania throughout their history. Greek mythology is filled with stories of magical contact with Egypt, and early Greek philosophers like Thales and Pythagoras were said to have derived the impetus for their intellectual inquiries from the knowledge they gained in Egypt. The fifth century B.C.E. historian Herodotus devotes an entire book in his *Histories* of the wars between Greeks and Persians to the history and culture of Egypt, where he probably traveled. Like most Greeks, Herodotus held a deep respect for the antiquity and vast knowledge of ancient Egypt.

After Alexander the Great's death, the 200-year rule of Egypt by the Greek Ptolemies from 332 to 331 B.C.E. both spread Greek influence into Egypt and helped to extend knowledge of Egypt into the Greek and subsequently Roman worlds. Thus, worship of the Egyptian goddess Isis, whose temple is found in the Hellenistic city on the Greek island of Delos, had by the Roman period spread to northern England.

The effect of Egyptomania was particularly prevalent during the Roman period. The Romans were fascinated with the ancient culture of Egypt, the religion above all, despite the fact that it was reviled and, often, defiled. The cult of Osiris and Isis was reborn as the cult of Osiris-Serapis and Isis, and this cult spread throughout the Mediterranean basin. Statues were carved in the Roman style wearing togas and having the current Roman hairstyles, while carrying ancient Egyptian icons related to the specific deities. Romans took antiquities from Egypt that they installed in the villas and estates of their most prominent senators and emperors. This period also witnessed a profusion of Roman tourists who left graffiti of their visits upon the pyramids.

Modern

Perhaps the first major modern expedition to bring ancient Egypt to Europe was Napoleon Bonaparte's attempt to conquer Egypt in 1798. Not intended simply as an invasion with an armada of warships with soldiers, Napoleon included savants in the complement. These savants were learned and knowledgeable men whose numbers included chemists, geometricians, mathematicians, naturalists, mineralogists, linguists, and artists, charged with the duty of recording Egypt. In all, the expedition took 151 nonmilitary personnel, in a specially appointed *Commission des Sciences et Arts*, or Commission of the Sciences and Arts. They were charged with recording as much of Egypt as possible, in the interests of the advancement of learning, a task in keeping with the Period of Enlightenment. The invasion lasted only 3 years, until 1801, but out of the short-lived mission came the *Description de l'Égypte* or *Description of Egypt* (1809–1828), a monumental set of nine volumes of text, ten albums of plates, and three volumes of maps and atlases. The first five volumes of albums of plates were devoted to Egyptian antiquities. Up until this, Egypt had been the interest of a relatively small portion of the population, scholars and scientists tucked away in universities throughout Europe. With the publication of the *Description de l'Égypte*, the artistic sensibilities of Egypt were made more widely available, and as a result, Egyptian motifs and styles became the rage for interior-decorating through Europe during the Napoleonic era, and Egyptomania as a style of design was born.

For Egyptology as a discipline, perhaps the most important discovery by Napoleon's army in Egypt was the Rosetta Stone, a trilingual stela from the Ptolemaic period, when Greece ruled Egypt. The languages included Greek and Egyptian hieroglyphs. This meant that it was possible for Champollion to compare Greek, a known ancient language, with the hieroglyphs and work out, from one of the king's names, the rest of the signs, and from there, the beginnings of the grammar. Suddenly, the words, thoughts, and deeds of the ancient Egyptians were available; they no longer belonged to some shadowy and mysterious world. With much of the vocabulary and grammar understood, most of the literature became available for general modern consumption. The exception to this is the religious literature, which, like most religious literature, requires a personal understanding of the ancient Egyptian faith that will always elude modern scholars. While some of the hymns to deities, the myths, as well as the basic language, are readily understood, much remains that entices with its impregnability.

The next significant event in bringing Egypt to the notice of the world was the discovery and opening of Tutankhamun's Eighteenth Dynasty tomb in the Valley of the Kings by Howard Carter in 1922. According to the news accounts of the day, the world held its collective breath while the stunning treasures from the tomb of a relatively unimportant king were catalogued and removed. Suddenly ancient Egypt became real to more than the Egyptologists and imaginations became fired in a completely new way. Carter's excavations reintroduced ancient Egypt to mainstream Europe, and in doing so, rekindled Egyptomania.

Between the discovery of Napoleon's savants in the late eighteenth century and the discovery of Tutankhamun's tomb in the early twentieth, the architects and interior decorators of Europe were incorporating Egyptian motifs into anything and everything. The European style of Egyptomania included antiquities, like the Roman, but it was more concerned with style and incorporating Egyptian elements into already-present European styles. The artists and architects created an Egyptianized look to interiors and exteriors, rather than the wholesale removal of Egypt to the Continent. Manufacturers such as Sévres, Wedgwood, Cartier, Baccarat, Piranesi, and Tiffany all contributed to the movement with completely original derivations of Egyptian motifs on dessert services, dinner settings, jewellery, sculpture, statues, lamps, perfume bottles, and tea pots. Entire rooms in the houses of the wealthiest people throughout Europe were devoted to Egyptian design, from floor to ceiling, including statues, and pyloned and columned entrances. These and many other aspects of decorative design featured new and innovative ways of looking at and using Egyptian elements of design.

While the fires of that particular style of design have died down considerably, it is still possible to find Egyptian decorative motifs in modern architecture and interior design. Two very good examples of this are the new court building on the east bank road or corniche in south Cairo, and the Luxor Hotel in Las Vegas, Nevada. The court building in Cairo has been built to scale as an Egyptian temple, and is one of the most imposing buildings along that part of the river, providing an updated version of the view that is now millennia old. On a much less serious note, the Luxor Hotel is itself enormous, and also built to scale, but it makes no claims for being imposing. It trades on the attraction of ancient Egypt, selling souvenirs that can only be described as kitsch in the hotel's stores. This whole-hearted acceptance of ancient Egypt into world architecture can be seen everywhere. Images of the pyramids abound—the glass entrance to the Louvre by the architect, I.M. Pei, the Pyramid Arena in Memphis, Tennessee, the above-mentioned Luxor Hotel, and many more. It has been assumed as a world cultural icon that carries with it the fascination of ancient Egypt settled into entirely new and unfamiliar but very successful circumstances.

MODERN PERCEPTIONS AND MISPERCEPTIONS

As the only one of the seven wonders of the ancient world left standing, and as some of the largest man-made structures in the world, the pyramids have long commanded more attention than any other antiquity in Egypt, large or small. Their size, the apparent mystery of their construction, and the enticement of the mere possibility of great riches within have all contributed to this popularity. In 1979, the pyramid fields from Giza to Dahshur were granted World Heritage status on the basis of several criteria—they represent masterpieces of human creative genius, they bear an exceptional testimony to a civilization that has disappeared, and they are directly associated with events, with beliefs, and with artistic works of outstanding universal significance. As World Heritage sites, their impact on the world is recognized, as well as standing as examples of the possibilities of human genius.

As the largest and best known of the entire corpus of pyramids, the pyramids of Giza carry with them a number of mental associations, some of which have been used by Hollywood in Biblical epics. One of the least savory of these is the vision of countless slave lives lost in their construction. The sheer size of the pyramids leads to this conclusion, and the mental image of thousands of men hauling enormous blocks of stone up precipitous and precarious sand ramps comes to the imagination. While very difficult to prove otherwise, this is a highly unlikely scenario. As mentioned in Chapter 5, the Giza plateau simply could not hold the hundreds of thousands of workers, nor was it to the benefit of the state to cause the deaths of vast portions of its working population, no matter what the cause. The work on the plateau and at other pyramid-building sites was difficult in the extreme, without argument, and it is certain that lives were lost. However, the cruelty of the Old Kingdom kings has yet to be proven definitively, and it flies in the face of available evidence. As such, it is most unlikely that regard for human life was not taken.

Together with a notion of a stunning loss of life on the ancient construction sites goes an awe at the enormity of the task. They set the standard for egomania on every level. The ability of the kings to command the labor, the materials, and the very construction of these enormous structures for the sole purpose of ensuring their continuing presence in the afterlife is beyond belief in today's world. This is accompanied, at times, by the belief that it was impossible for the pyramids to have been built through human labor, and simply put, that they were built by aliens. Other suggestions also surface, suggestions tied to the ostensible mystery of the pyramids, and the idea that the solution of those mysteries will provide us with the wisdom of the ancients. The presence of the pyramids in the human imagination is large, and fills many roles for many people. Enough archaeological evidence exists for Egyptologists largely to understand the construction and the meaning of the pyramids for the ancient Egyptians; today the meaning of the pyramids is different, and for the most part, equally valid. It is testimony to their place in world culture.

TOURIST ATTRACTIONS

The use of the pyramids as economic entities for modern Egypt must not be overlooked in a discussion of a modern interpretation. Egypt today survives largely as a result of the tourists that flock to see the various antiquities; it has been shown that the income from tourism is greater than that coming from exports of petroleum, telecommunications, textiles, or motor vehicles.[1] It provides over 2 million jobs, and for some, provides a very good living. Cairo University and Zagazig University in the Delta in particular both have prominent and active Egyptology departments, training Egyptians in the ancient history of their country, providing them with the wherewithal to work with expeditions and as researchers in museums throughout Egypt, as well as providing well-qualified guides for the tourist industry.

As tourism grows, so does its economic importance to Egypt and its inhabitants. Millions of tourists each year visit the antiquities in Alexandria, Cairo, Luxor, and Aswan. The numbers of people going through the pyramids and the tombs in the Valley of the Kings on the West Bank at Luxor, with all the humidity from their breath, the pounding of their footsteps, and the often careless attitude toward the fragility of the remains has led the Supreme Council of Antiquities of the Egyptian government to rotate the sites that are open to the public, or restrict the numbers of tourists allowed in each day. The latter is the situation for the pyramids on the Giza plateau, and those tombs in the Valley of the Kings that are open alternate three or four times during the year. Some tombs in the Valley of the Kings, such as that of Seti I, a Nineteenth Dynasty king, are closed permanently due to the frail condition of the reliefs and architecture, a most unfortunate circumstance for the most beautifully decorated tomb in the Valley. Another route taken by the Supreme Council of Antiquities is to charge steep entrance fees, such as that for the Twentieth Dynasty queen, Nefertari's tomb in the Valley of the Queens, which is approximately forty times the fee for other tombs in the Valley of the Kings and the Valley of the Queens.

The destruction of antiquities is of grave concern to the Egyptian government and to foreign expeditions alike. The threats from humidity and constant ground movement from footsteps are not the only worries, however. Graffiti is an ongoing concern, and more importantly, there is a thriving trade in illegal sale of antiquities, some of which is very sophisticated. Both native Egyptians and foreigners take part in these two activities. For Egyptologists, the greatest crime in this is the loss of information that accompanies the sale of any illegally gathered antiquity. Without knowing the provenance or site of origin of an antiquity, often it is impossible to tell to which age it belonged, to whom it belonged, and the other finds with which it was associated. As such, any unprovenanced antiquity is a thing of beauty and age, but also a thing without meaning or import. For modern Egyptians, it is a loss of their national heritage, a loss as important as that of information.

CONCLUSION

The culture of ancient Egypt, as seen through its remains, has had a deep-seated impact on both ancient and modern world culture. From the earliest periods of Western culture with the Greeks and then the Romans, the Egyptians have captivated popular imagination. A number of elements in particular have contributed to this—the great age of ancient Egyptian civilization, almost exactly 3,000 years; the huge stone monuments that remain; and the religion. The effect this has had on the public perception of the pyramids has been multifold. They have been inserted into popular imagination and thought as immense testaments to human ingenuity, creativity, and rampant egomania, as design motifs used in architecture and other artistic endeavors, and as tombs that once were filled with a now mythical amount of wealth. They have been understood to work in a variety of celestial ways other than simply as tombs, representing the possibilities of alien intervention in human affairs. Finally, they represent a modern means of making a living for Egyptians. These varying appreciations of the pyramids are certainly far from the original intent, but this is to be expected and perhaps, even relished. They have long outlived both their initial purpose and the civilization that built them. Consequently, it is conceivable that they should be accepted and understood in whatever light modern humanity sees fit.

NOTE

1. S. Tohamy and A. Swinscoe, "The Economic Impact of Tourism in Egypt," *Egyptian Center for Economic Studies*, Working Paper No. 40, June 2000, p. 3 (available at http://www.eldis.org/static/DOC11018.htm/)

PYRAMID PROFILES

The following profiles are presented in temporal order, from earliest in the Third Dynasty to latest in the Sixth.

PYRAMID NAME UNKNOWN, STEP PYRAMID (DJOSER, DYNASTY THREE)

Built at South Saqqara, this is the first attempt at a superstructural pyramid. It was built for the first king of the Third Dynasty, Djoser, by his architect, Imhotep. The entire complex comprises a "palace-façade" enclosure wall (ca. 597 yards north/south x 304 yards east/west), the six-layer Step Pyramid (204 feet high x 411 feet east/west x 358 feet north/south), and a number of other buildings not included in later pyramid complexes. These are as follows, from the southern end of the complex: the colonnade entrance, the south court, the south tomb and its chapel, three long massifs (known as the western massifs), which run along the western walls of the pyramid and enclosure, two boundary markers, which are part of the *heb-sed* buildings, an altar along the south wall of the pyramid, the *heb-sed* court and buildings, and temple T. The pavilions of the south and north lie between the eastern walls of the pyramid and the enclosure. Against the northern wall of the pyramid, there is a serdab with a court, and the northern temple. The northern third, approximately, of the enclosure is yet to be fully excavated; however in the northeastern corner, there is evidence of a ramp over the enclosure wall.

This is the earliest stone structure in Egypt, perhaps the world, and as such, it provides evidence of the first use of certain architectural forms that later became standards in the Egyptian architectural language. The colonnaded entrance is a very good example of this: the columns are only partially detached from the larger blocks of stone from which they were carved, causing them to look fully carved in the round from the corridor, while still retaining large portions of the original stone at the back. They are known as engaged columns. Undoubtedly this was done to provide stability, and is lithic evidence for the ongoing understanding of working in stone by the builders. The next pyramids, with their pyramid and valley temples, have fully detached columns, indicating the progress of the builders in the use of stone. The *heb-sed* buildings also show this lack of certainty concerning how far to cut stone while still maintaining its properties of strength. For the most part, the *heb-sed* buildings are thick-walled, with doors of stone that, while carved to appear able to shut, are immovable.

PYRAMID NAME UNKNOWN, MEIDUM (SNEFERU, DYNASTY FOUR)

The pyramid at Meidum of Sneferu is the first attempt at a smooth-sided pyramid, although ultimately it was unsuccessful. All that is visible today is the inner core of the original step pyramid with three steps above the sand and surrounding debris. The outer layers have sloughed off and lie in ruins around the base of the core; however, within that debris, excavators have found that it was built originally as a pyramid of seven steps, after which it was enlarged with an outer covering, giving it eight steps. Then at some point, it was further remodeled with smooth sides. The final measurements were a height of 302 feet, with a base of 473 feet. The burial chamber has a corbelled ceiling, and is at ground level. A passage leads from approximately 54 feet up the north side down through the pyramid to a site just below the burial chamber, a distance of approximately 221 feet The burial chamber is reached through a vertical shaft about 21 feet in length. Logs are fitted into the ceiling of the corbelled ceiling from side to side across the expanse of the room, and it is likely these were to have been used to lift the sarcophagus into position, had the pyramid actually been used for the use for which it was intended.

Only faint traces remain of an enclosure wall, not enough to give an indication of original size. The pyramid was equipped with a fairly rudimentary funerary chapel (34 feet square x 9 feet high) on the east side. The funerary chapel had three rooms, with offset entrances to each room, ensuring that the innermost one, the holiest, could not be glimpsed from outside the building. Within this room, the excavators found two tall slabs of limestone with rounded tops on either side of an altar. Unfortunately, these slabs were without inscriptions, although their use in a funerary context is clear.

On the north side of the pyramid next to the enclosure wall, a mastaba was built, although it has now disappeared. The placement of the mastaba within the pyramid complex was unusual, although the earlier Step Pyramid of Djoser at Saqqara also had a mastaba in the precinct, in the southwest corner.

The causeway begins about 80 feet from the entrance of the funerary chapel. It was built with limestone walls, and although it is a well-made piece of architecture, it doesn't lead to a valley temple, but rather, ends quite abruptly. The floor of the causeway was carved out of the bedrock and paved with mud.

"SNEFERU SHINES," DAHSHUR SOUTH (SNEFERU, DYNASTY FOUR)

Sneferu built his next pyramid 21 miles north of Meidum, at Dahshur. Both this pyramid and the North Pyramid at Dahshur were called "Sneferu Shines." This is known today as the Bent Pyramid, due to a change in the angle of the courses. The full height of the pyramid is 345 feet with a base of 617 feet. At about 112 feet, the slope changed from 54° 27′ 44″ to 43° 22′, a much steeper angle designed to lower the ultimate height of the building. Evidence of structural damage due to subsidence has been found, indicating the reason for the change in angle. Despite this, however, the Bent Pyramid has more of the outer casing preserved than any other pyramid, giving some indication of what the pyramids must have looked like originally.

Uniquely in the Old Kingdom, there are entrances on two sides of the pyramid, the north and the west, and each corridor leads to a separate chamber, the lower of the two, the antechamber, was cut into the bedrock. The northern entrance, about 39 feet up, leads down a steep, narrow corridor for about 245 feet, whereupon it becomes almost like a foyer with a corbelled ceiling. This leads ultimately to a chamber that seems to have functioned as a storage or antechamber. The western entrance lies about 110 feet from the ground near the middle of the west face. This leads for 278 feet to another chamber, higher than the antechamber, but not immediately above it. Both chambers have corbelled ceilings. It is due to the presence of a block with Sneferu's name on it found below the floor of the upper chamber that this chamber is considered to be the burial chamber; however, no trace of a sarcophagus was found in either chamber.

About 60 yards to the south of the pyramid, a satellite pyramid was built, 174 feet at its base with a height of 107 feet. It has a small chamber accessed by a corridor, the entrance of which is in the center of the north face. A small chapel was built in front of the north face and two round-topped stelae were placed against the west face. The enclosure wall that surrounds the entire complex makes a detour around this small pyramid.

Against the main pyramid's west side, a chapel was built, simpler even than that at Meidum, having only one room with an entrance corridor. As at Meidum, however, the doors are not set in a line—the corridor's entrance is to the south, the room's is to the east—to ensure that no one could look straight into the chapel. Again as at Meidum, the chapel contains an altar, on either side of which are two stelae, only stumps of which remain.

The causeway leads 689 feet at an angle from the north side of the enclosure wall to a valley temple, the earliest yet to be discovered. The north wall of the causeway stops when it reaches the southwest corner of the temple, but the south wall of the causeway continues across the entrance, to hide the interior of the building from the uninitiated. Two stelae were erected outside this wall at each of the corners. The stelae have *serekhs* on them with figures of the seated king, surrounded by his titles. Beneath this, there is a palace façade, and above the whole *serekh*-rectangle is a large figure of the Horus falcon.

Rectangular in shape, and entered from the south, the temple contained a series of four narrow rectangular storage rooms running perpendicular to the entrance. A hallway from the entrance goes between them and leads to an open courtyard with two rows of five rectangular pillars at the north end. These pillars are in front of six statues, of Sneferu striding forth, in a row against the north wall. The inner walls of the courtyard are decorated with scenes of personified estates bringing offerings to the king.

"SNEFERU SHINES," DAHSHUR NORTH (SNEFERU, DYNASTY FOUR)

The so-called Red Pyramid at Dahshur is the first true pyramid, smooth-sided without a change in angle. The name comes not from the outer color of the stone, but rather from the faint pinkish hue of the limestone inside the chambers. It was named "Sneferu Shines" when it was built, as was the Bent or South Pyramid. Begun in around Sneferu's thirtieth year on the throne, it was his final attempt at pyramid-building, although he did return to the first pyramid at Meidum to remake the tomb into a true pyramid, and the second to complete the structure. For some time, the attribution of the pyramid was in doubt, until the excavator discovered a block with the name and date of Sneferu on it that had tumbled from the upper portions of east face. When the Red Pyramid was complete, it stood approximately 353 feet high, and the base was approximately 722 feet on each side. It has a relatively gentle slope, closer to that of the upper part of the Bent Pyramid, than to later pyramids. As with the earlier pyramids, the chambers remain close to ground level, if not actually on the ground. The burial chamber was built in a similar manner to the Bent Pyramid, on a higher level than the two entrance chambers. The entrance of the passageway to the chambers lies about 94 feet above the ground and runs down to the center of the pyramid for about 231 feet. The chambers have corbelled ceilings, without the wooden crossbars necessary in the Bent Pyramid.

The Red Pyramid complex appears to have been finished in a hurry, probably due to the king's ill health, or even imminent death. It has a complete enclosure wall and a mortuary temple against the east face of the pyramid, but the temple is small and rudimentary, while the southern half of the eastern wall appears to have been begun at a turn several meters to the west of the northern corner. This means that the southern half abuts the mortuary temple and goes around it, rather than meeting the northern half in front of the temple. There are two stone chapels on either side of the mortuary temple entrance, the entranceway between them leading to an inner sanctuary. The remains of holes dug for planting trees and other flora were discovered north and south of the temple walls.

There is no sign of a substantial causeway but there was a valley temple, in which was found the decree by Pepi I of the Sixth Dynasty, exempting temple workers from the corvée. The valley temple has never been properly excavated.

"HORIZON OF KHUFU," GIZA PLATEAU (KHUFU, DYNASTY FOUR)

The Great Pyramid at Giza is the largest of all the pyramids built in Egypt, despite the fact that to the human eye, the pyramid next to it appears larger. It was given the name *Akhet Khufu* or Horizon of Khufu. It measured 481 feet in height and its base was 756 feet. It is merely 3 feet 6 inches off true north, a truly astonishingly minute amount of variation given the surveying tools of the time. The base is level to within 1 inch, and the greatest length difference in the sides is 1.75 inches. The pyramid itself contains approximately 2,300,000 blocks of stone that each weigh on average about 2.5 tons. The complex of Khufu's pyramid includes the enclosure wall, mortuary temple, causeway, and valley temple that are now standard, but it also included pyramids for three queens, seven boat pits, and a satellite pyramid. Everything to do with this pyramid was a significant step up from previous pyramids, from size to complexity of the mortuary temple.

One of the most significant differences was the placement of the burial chamber in the middle of the pyramid rather than at ground level, which is itself a significant feat of engineering. The interior chambers are considerably more complicated than those of earlier pyramids. The entrance is in the north face at 55 feet above ground level and it bifurcates approximately 60 feet into the pyramid into an Ascending Passage and a Descending Passage. The Ascending Passage leads to the Grand Gallery and further, to the King's Chamber. At the beginning of the Grand Gallery, the Ascending Passage again bifurcates and continues as the Horizontal Passage to the so-called Queen's Chamber. Air shafts rise from both the King's and the Queen's Chambers to the north and the south faces. The Ascending Passage and the Descending Passage are connected by a "shaft" or "well" that runs from the beginning of the Grand Gallery to several yards from the entrance to the Subterranean Chamber.

The King's Chamber, in particular, is another engineering marvel. Above the chamber are five "relieving chambers," one above the other, and separated by a slab of limestone. They were incorporated into the structure to ease the weight on the King's Chamber from above. The highest of these chambers has a tent-shaped ceiling that serves to distribute the weight to either side of the chambers below.

The Queen's Chamber has undoubtedly been misnamed by modern scholars, as it is far too small to have accommodated the burial of a queen. Rather, it was probably a storage room or a sealed room for a special "soul" statue of the king.

The Grand Gallery is a beautiful room, with a 26 foot ceiling and gently corbelling walls, although the ceiling itself was finished by great limestone slabs. The reason for the Grand Gallery is unknown, although a number of speculations have been put forward. One opinion is the Gallery was used as an alleyway to bring blocks up through the center of the pyramid; another is that it served some sort of ritual function. There is no archaeological evidence for either of these, nor is there evidence for any other hypothesis. It seems likely to remain a mystery.

Continuing down the entranceway past the beginning of the Ascending Passage, the Descending Passage begins and reaches a Subterranean Chamber after approximately 192 feet. The Subterranean Chamber appears to be unfinished; the ceiling was completed, but the floor wasn't, and is very rough.

The enclosure wall that surrounded the pyramid complex was over 26 feet high. Unlike earlier pyramids, the mortuary temple was not enclosed within the wall, but was incorporated into it on the north side. A covered causeway led to the valley temple, which was discovered relatively recently, as noted in Chapter Three.

Two of the boat pits, those on the south side, contained the remains of real, life-sized boats. They were originally covered by limestone slabs. The first boat pit to be opened was the one to the east. The boat within it was removed and reassembled, and is now held in the Boat Museum next to the pyramid. The ship was found in 1,224 pieces, which made up 656 major portions. It was originally held together with rope, making reassembly possible. When in the water, the rope would swell and pull the pieces together, making it watertight. The hull contains a number of sections held together with mortice and tenon joints. The length of the boat is 142 feet, and it is 19 feet at its widest.

The second boat pit seems to be shorter than the boat would have been when assembled. This boat has not been moved, although it is certain that another disassembled boat is under the limestone-block roof, as an investigation with a tiny camera through a hole drilled in the ceiling has shown.

Khufu built three pyramids for his queens, although which queens they were is still up for debate. It has been theorized that the northern-most belonged to Hetepheres, the wife of Sneferu and possibly Khufu's mother, and that the one furthest south belonged to Henutsen. The owner of the middle pyramid has not been identified, even in theory. Each of the pyramids had a passageway that sloped down to a burial chamber, but nothing was found in the chambers. Queen Hetepheres' furniture was found, however, buried in a small chamber on the north side. It was discovered in 1925 by the photographer of the American expedition then excavating there. He was setting up a tripod when one leg sank into the sand and stopped with a hollow sound, whereupon a shaft was discovered containing the queen's bed with canopy, a carrying chair, two sitting chairs, a curtain box, and a number of vessels. These have been reconstructed and can be seen in the Cairo Museum.

PYRAMID NAME UNKNOWN, ABU ROASH (DJEDEFRE, DYNASTY FOUR)

For an unknown reason, the next king of Dynasty Four, Djedefre, a son of Khufu, chose to move the site of his pyramid north 5 miles to Abu Roash. In placement, it is almost directly across, as the crow flies, from Heliopolis, one possible reason for the removal to this site. Very little is left of this pyramid, other than a core of limestone and a few blocks surrounding it; it does not seem to have been finished. Despite the ruination, however, it is possible to discern that it was probably 348 feet per side, and anywhere from 187 to 220 feet in height.

When it was built, the complex contained a pyramid within an enclosure wall, with a satellite pyramid in the southwest corner. The remains of an entrance passageway have been found, and it leads to a shaft, rather than a burial chamber. The shaft is approximately 66 feet deep, and the passageway is 161 feet long. The mortuary temple is shifted slightly north of the east/west axis and it is relatively complex with a large number of rooms. Just to the south of the temple is a boat pit. The causeway is very long, at 5,577 feet. Undoubtedly, this was in order to reach the pyramid, which was placed on quite a high plateau, from which Giza is visible in the distance.

"GREAT IS KHAFRE," GIZA PLATEAU (KHAFRE, DYNASTY FOUR)

The middle pyramid on the Giza Plateau is that built by Khafre, another son of Khufu. It appears to be the largest, but in this case, appearances are deceptive, as it was built on a level of bedrock 33 feet higher than Khufu's. Its name was *Wer Khafre* or "Great is Khafre." Its height was 471 feet, and its base ran along 705 feet. The top of the pyramid still has the original limestone casings, a feature that makes it readily identifiable.

The interior is much simpler in design than Khufu's with one burial chamber and one subsidiary chamber near the entrance. These chambers are at or below ground level. There were two entrances, built into the same northern side, one upper and the other lower. The higher entrance was situated about 38 feet above ground level, while the lower passage begins at ground level. The passageways leading from these meet at a horizontal level and lead to the burial chamber. The smaller subsidiary chamber is off the lower of the two passages.

An enclosure wall surrounds the whole, with the mortuary temple creating a break in it on the eastern side. A satellite pyramid lies outside the wall on the southern side, but it has been so denuded and robbed of stone that attribution is impossible. A causeway leads from the mortuary temple, past the Sphinx, to a valley temple, which lies next to a temple dedicated to the Sphinx.

The mortuary temple is the largest yet seen, and for the first time, contains all the elements that were later to become standard: an entrance hall, a columned court, five niches for statues of the king, five storage chambers, and an inner sanctuary that contained a pair of stelae and/or a false door. It was built generally in two sections, with the entrance way and storage chambers in the first section, and the niches and sanctuary in the second. The valley temple, one of the best preserved of any valley temple, has an entrance hall and a columned court, much like any entranceway to a grand Egyptian house.

The Sphinx was built during Khafre's reign, and is likely a portrait of the king. It was sculpted from bedrock, and over the millennia, it has been restored by several kings and organizations. The first restoration was during the Eighteenth Dynasty, the next probably during the Twenty-Sixth Dynasty. It was again restored during the Graeco-Roman period, and again, by modern restorers in the 1920s, the 1940s, and the

1960s–1970s. The body is that of a lion, while the head is human, and wears a headdress particular to royalty in ancient Egypt. The Egyptians left two cave-like pockets, under the rump of the sculpture and under what would have been the center. There is nothing to suggest that these were anything but natural fissures in the rock.

"MENKAURE IS DIVINE," GIZA PLATEAU (MENKAURE, DYNASTY FOUR)

Menkaure's pyramid is the smallest on the Giza Plateau, but in many ways, it is the most interesting. It contains a much more complex interior chamber system, including a paneled chamber that was the first in a pyramid since Djoser's Step Pyramid. It was unfinished, although there was not much work left to do. It was only about 213 feet high, and its base area was 335 x 343 feet. Its name was *Netjeri Menkaure* or "Menkaure is Divine."

The top of the pyramid was dressed in the usual fine limestone, but the lowest sixteen courses were composed of red granite, a much harder stone. The granite faces were not finished, with the exception of a few places around the entrance. The entrance is in the north side of the pyramid, approximately 13 feet above ground level. It descends for 102 feet to a paneled chamber. A doorway on the opposite side from the entrance passage in this chamber was blocked by three portcullis blocks. Past these, a further passage led to an antechamber. In the middle of the antechamber floor, another descending passage led down to another chamber that had six niches, perhaps for statues of the king. Yet another short corridor led from the antechamber through another smaller room to the burial chamber. At one time, this contained a sarcophagus of a dark stone, carved in paneling along all four outer walls. It was removed in the early twentieth century and packed aboard a ship bound for England. The ship sank on the voyage and the sarcophagus was lost. The very complexity of the rooms' arrangement within the pyramid, the paneling, and the niched room all suggest a hearkening back to the Step Pyramid of Djoser, and perhaps a deliberate archaizing as homage to an earlier king.

The mortuary temple and causeway betray most strongly the fact that the king died before the complex was finished. Both were only partially finished in stone, and then finished in mudbrick, probably by Menkaure's successor as quickly as possible. The causeway was in fact not even completely finished in mudbrick, but left part way to act merely as a road for the delivery of stone.

The valley temple was relatively small, with an entrance, flanked by eight rectangular rooms. The entrance led into an open court. At the opposite side of the court another entrance led to the inner sanctuary, flanked itself by magazines on the north and other rooms, perhaps ritual in nature, to the south. In this temple, in the rooms to the south of the sanctuary, the excavator found a statue of the king and his queen (a dyad), and several of the king and two female deities (a triad), which are among the most beautiful works of art in the world today.

Three queens' pyramids lie to the south of Menkaure's complex. The two westernmost are in the shape of step pyramids, and were either built as such deliberately, or were unfinished and betray a building process frozen in time. It seems likely that they were intended specifically as queens' pyramids; the middle one had the body of a young woman in the burial chamber.

"PURE ARE THE PLACES OF USERKAF," SAQQARA (USERKAF, DYNASTY FIVE)

From Giza, where there was no room left for any further pyramid building, Userkaf, the first king of Dynasty Five, moved his pyramid site to Saqqara. He chose to build it as close to Djoser's Step Pyramid complex as possible, just off its southwest corner. Today the pyramid is barely recognizable as a pyramid, it is so denuded. When the limestone casing was removed, the core masonry was so poorly constructed that it fell apart. It was also much smaller than previous pyramids, being only 161 feet in height when it was complete. The base was 240 feet. This might have been due to the fact that his reign was very short, probably only 7 or 8 years long.

The entrance was set into the north face, although it is too destroyed to say at what level. A passage of 61 feet in length descended to a passage described as a construction passage, possibly similar in intent to Khufu's Grand Gallery. This passage had portcullises on the southern end, past which was an L-shaped collection of chambers. The construction passage led directly to the antechamber and a short passage led west to the burial chamber. Just ahead of the antechamber's entrance, another short passage led to a magazine or storage room, in the north wall of which was the entrance to another rectangular room.

Userkaf's offering chapel is against the east face of the pyramid, while, most unusually, the mortuary temple is included in the enclosure wall, on the south side. This may be due to the proximity to Djoser's pyramid. A satellite pyramid lies in the southwest corner of the enclosure. A causeway leads from the southeastern corner of the complex. The entire layout of the mortuary temple is odd, undoubtedly to account for its unique positioning. The causeway leads to a foyer to the south of which are a series of magazines. Following the foyer north, it turns into another entranceway that leads itself into a columned open courtyard. South of this are the five statue niches and columns in front of them.

Just to the south of the complex, Userkaf built a pyramid, probably for a queen. It had an empty burial chamber, as well as a mortuary temple.

"THE RISING OF THE *BA* SPIRIT," ABUSIR (SAHURE, DYNASTY FIVE)

The pyramid of Sahure marks yet another change of location, this time to Abusir, which remained the royal necropolis for the next two kings of the Fifth Dynasty. As with most of the pyramids after those on the Giza Plateau, Sahure's is in a state of ruin. The limestone outer casings have been removed, and what remains looks like a mere jumble of stones. The core of the pyramid was constructed of blocks of limestone, roughly shaped into five or six steps and held together with mud mortar. An opening in the north side was left for workers to complete the interior chambers while construction went on around. At the completion of the chambers, the gap was filled with construction debris. When new, it was 154 feet high, with a base of 258 feet square. The mortuary temple was more complex than any other (see Document 4 for an inscription from the temple), and the valley temple has been found, close to what might be the wall of the pyramid town, named "The Soul of Sahure Comes Forth in Glory."

The pyramid itself was entered from a passageway set near ground level in the north face. The interior plan of the pyramid was simple with one passage leading to the burial chamber, but it was badly damaged, and only one fragment was left from the basalt sarcophagus.

The mortuary temple, while more complex than earlier temples, had the five elements, first found in Khafre's temple and now expected in such buildings: entrance hall, open court, five niches for statues, magazines, and sanctuary. As with earlier examples, the mortuary temple was incorporated into the enclosure wall and was placed against the eastern face of the pyramid. What separates this mortuary temple from earlier examples is the amount and fine artistry of the artwork in relief that decorated the walls. They remain some of the finest reliefwork done in ancient Egypt, and contain a wide variety of scenes from the king's life. They include scenes showing massive numbers of cattle and other animals (123,400 head of cattle, 223,400 asses, 232,413 deer, and 243,688 sheep) being presented to the king as booty from foreign wars, as well as marvelously idiosyncratic hunting scenes with the king and his courtiers standing in the desert, while a jerboa and a hedgehog disappear down their holes.

The causeway, 775 feet long, led from the entrance to the mortuary temple straight to the valley temple. The causeway was also decorated in the finest reliefs, as were earlier causeways. The quality of the reliefwork in Sahure's causeway, however, far surpasses that of other examples, with scenes of foreign prisoners being brought before the king.

The valley temple was set on the shore of a lake that was present during this period. Two landing ramps have been found, one to the east and one to the south. Again, the walls of the valley temple were covered with reliefwork. The eastern landing ramp led straight into the structure that was fronted by a columned portico. This led then into a hall with two columns in it, which finally led to the causeway.

Architecturally, this entire complex differed from others in the use of an elaborate system of drainage, using stone spouts in the shape of lions' heads projecting from the tops of the walls. Water was led away from the building through a system of openings in the base of the outer walls and from there, it was directed into a series of channels cut into the paving. For ritually pure water used in ceremonies, copper-lined stone basins were used with lead plugs as stoppers. These were connected to copper pipes that led to an underground drainage system that ran beneath the entire complex until it reached the end of the causeway by the valley temple.

"PYRAMID OF THE *BA* OF NEFERIRKARE," ABUSIR (NEFERIRKARE, DYNASTY FIVE)

The pyramid of Neferirkare was larger than that of his brother, Sahure, and it had a slightly more complex interior collection of rooms than did

Sahure's. The pyramid was not finished, however, and it was left as a six-step pyramid that was intended to have been finished as a true pyramid at a later date. The height would have been 236 feet when finished, and the base was 344 feet. Neferirkare's valley temple and causeway were usurped by his successor, Niuserre.

The interior of the pyramid was reached by a descending passage that led to two small fore-chambers. Another passage, horizontal, led to an antechamber. Through a short passage cut into the west wall of the antechamber, one reached the burial chamber. Each chamber had ceilings of very thick limestone blocks that distributed the weight to either side. The burial chamber had three such levels.

The mortuary temple was on the eastern side and consisted of a columned entrance hall that led to an open courtyard with columns around the perimeter. Entrances led through the west wall of the courtyard into the statue area and behind that, the inner sanctuary. One of the most important caches of papyri, known now as the Abusir Papyri, was found in the mortuary temple. These papyri are primarily concerned with the day-to-day working of the mortuary temple cult, and provide a fascinating, otherwise lost, glimpse into a more human facet of the pyramid complexes.

Only the foundations of the causeway and valley temple were finished before the king died.

PYRAMID NAME UNKNOWN, ABUSIR (RANEFEREF [A.K.A. NEFEREFRE], DYNASTY FIVE)

Raneferef seems to have died shortly after the beginning of construction on his pyramid, because all that remains is a ramp down to what appears to be the beginning of construction on a chamber; these, however, are completely gone. It is impossible, therefore, to say how tall it would have stood, but the base seems to have been begun with 213 feet, meaning it would have been of a reasonable size, similar to that of Sahure's.

His mortuary temple was in an L-shape, due to the presence of an entrance hall and a "Sanctuary of the Knife," an area for ritually sacrificing animals for offerings in the daily cult. These two sections were added later on to the front of the building, the entrance hall built in the center and the "Sanctuary" to the south. At the south end of the original temple is a large court that once held wooden columns; this was Egypt's first hypostyle hall, which is a hall filled with columns such as is found at the much-later temple of Karnak. As with nearly all pyramids, the mortuary temple as a whole was against what would have been the east face of the pyramid.

"THE PLACES OF NIUSERRE ENDURE," ABUSIR (NIUSERRE, DYNASTY FIVE)

Niuserre was the last king of Dynasty Five to build his pyramid complex at Abusir. He was on the throne for more than 30 years, which enabled him to complete his complex. The pyramid was 259 feet square at the base and stood 164 feet high. The core of the pyramid was a step pyramid, later remodeled as a true pyramid. As with many other pyramids, the casing of Niuserre's has been robbed, leaving only the core. He usurped his father, Neferirkare's causeway and valley temple foundations. He angled the beginning of his causeway to the south to meet up with what had been completed of his father's.

The entrance is at ground level on the northern side. The passage leads down to a foyer which has an ascending ceiling. Just past this passage are three portcullis gates. Past these, another passage leads to the antechamber, and as has become the norm, a short passage in the antechamber's western wall leads to the burial chamber. Similarly to Neferirkare's chamber ceilings, Niuserre's are three levels of limestone beams. Each of these limestone beams is 33 feet long and weighs 90 tons.

The pyramid is enclosed by a wall, which is interrupted at the southeast corner by the mortuary temple. South of the mortuary temple and attached to the enclosure wall is a satellite pyramid. At the southeast and northeast corners of the enclosure wall are structures that appear to be forerunners of the pylon gates that fronted Eighteenth Dynasty temples. The entrance hall is flanked by magazines and leads to an open court that was columned around the sides. The rest of the mortuary temple was built at right angles to the entrance areas, and against the east face of the pyramid. The reason for the right angle was to avoid mastabas, which had been built just in front of the pyramid.

The causeway led to a valley temple. The temple had a landing ramp that led up to a porticoed hallway, which itself led through to a room with three niches. Through the north side of this niched room, another room led to the causeway entrance.

"BEAUTIFUL IS ISESI," SOUTH SAQQARA (DJEDKARE-ISESI, DYNASTY FIVE)

Djedkare-Isesi chose to build his pyramid complex at South Saqqara. It had a base length of 258 feet and a finished height of 172 feet. It was partially destroyed in antiquity, and as a result, it can be seen that it began as a stepped structure, later given straight sides.

The pyramid has an entrance in the east side at ground level, and the entrance passage leads to a foyer-type of corridor. Past this foyer lie three portcullises, and past these is the antechamber with the burial chamber to the west. East of the antechamber, for the first time, is a room with three niches or magazines, a feature that will become standard in the rest of the Old Kingdom pyramids. This room is sometimes known as the serdab.

An enclosure wall circles the complex. The mortuary temple, against the east face of the pyramid is constructed as two separate parts, with an entrance hall, flanked by magazines, leading into an open court surrounded by columns. The open court leads into a long transverse hallway that separates this front section from the statue room and sanctuary in the back section. A satellite pyramid was built beside the back section. On either side of the entrance hall in the front section are the pylons earlier seen in Niuserre's complex. An unexcavated causeway leads down to the modern village of Saqqara, under which there may be a valley temple.

To the north of the first section of mortuary temple, Djedkare-Isesi built a satellite pyramid for his queen with the standard features of a king's pyramid complex, on a much smaller scale. This included a satellite pyramid. This is the first time a queen has been granted the full complex.

"PERFECT ARE THE PLACES OF UNAS," SOUTH SAQQARA (UNAS, DYNASTY FIVE)

Unas' pyramid complex is off the southwest corner of Djoser's at South Saqqara. Blocks from the Step Pyramid enclosure were used to plug gaps in the ground when Unas' causeway was built, indicating that by this time, Djoser's complex was already falling into ruin. Although his causeway is the best preserved of any, Unas' pyramid has not faired any better. The core was made of small limestone blocks and mud mortar. The base was 189 feet square, and the height was 141 feet. The interior chamber system is simple, and similar to earlier ones with one major, groundbreaking exception, and that is the decoration of the entranceway, the antechamber, and the burial chamber with Pyramid Texts.

The entrance is located on the north side at ground level under the face of the pavement. There are signs of a building over the entrance in the form of a chapel. The passage descends for about 33 feet before reaching a chamber much like a foyer built into the passage. Past this were three portcullises. The passageway continued into the antechamber, which had a short passage off the west side to the burial chamber. As in Djedkare-Isesi's pyramid chamber system, Unas also has a room with three niches or magazines, called a serdab, to the east of the antechamber, connected to it by a short passage. The Pyramid Texts begin before the corridor chamber or foyer and continue down the walls of the passageway, into the antechamber and burial chamber. The only room not decorated was the niched room. Around the sarcophagus in the burial chamber, the walls to approximately 3 feet were decorated with reeds, as if in a marsh, which created the image of the sarcophagus as the Primeval Mound rising from the waters. Above the reeds, the Pyramid Texts relating to the daily offerings surrounded the sarcophagus area.

The rest of the complex is much as previous ones, although on a slightly smaller scale. The mortuary complex, against the east side of the pyramid, began with an entrance hall flanked by magazines for storage. The hall opened into an open court with columns around the perimeter. As with Djedkare-Isesi's mortuary temple, Unas' front section was divided from the back section by a transverse hallway. Through this, one entered the back section, into the room with five statue niches, and then into the sanctuary. A satellite pyramid was located to the south of the transverse corridor. The causeway led 2,460 feet to the valley temple. Two entrances to the valley temple led from the waterway, the main one to the portico and the rest of the temple.

The causeway deserves comment. As it is the best preserved of any other Old Kingdom causeway, enough remains to give a good picture of what the causeways in general must have looked like. The full height of the walls remains in one section of Unas', with roofing slabs that leave a narrow gap between them in the middle of the ceiling. This allowed light to enter and make the marvelous carved and painted reliefs on the walls to be visible. The reliefs contained scenes of warfare, hunting, craftsmen, transportation ships, wild animals, foreign prisoners, the previously mentioned starving Bedouin, estate workers, and offering bearers.

During the New Kingdom, in the Nineteenth Dynasty, a son of Ramesses II, Khaemwaset, was particularly interested in his country's past—he has been called the world's first historian and archaeologist. He restored a number of ancient, even to him, buildings, one of which was Unas' pyramid. He left an inscription noting this work on the south face, saying that he had caused Unas' name to live again.

"THE PLACES OF TETI ENDURE," NORTH SAQQARA (TETI, DYNASTY SIX)

Despite the fact that Manetho divides the Fifth and Sixth Dynasties after Unas, there seems to be no reason to have done so. This is particularly evident when the pyramids' interiors and complexes are compared. The pyramid itself was given a stepped core, and was filled with small limestone blocks and debris. Each side of Teti's pyramid was 258 feet, and it rose to a height of 172 feet, measuring slightly larger than Unas'.

The entrance to the pyramid is on the north side of the pyramid, with a small chapel-type building on top of it. The short descending corridor leads to a foyer, past three portcullises, to an antechamber with the burial chamber accessed from the west wall of the antechamber. A serdab lies to the east of the antechamber. The ante- and burial chambers are roofed with three tiers of massive limestone blocks.

Teti's pyramid chambers and entrance passages are carved with the Pyramid Texts, as are the rest of the pyramids from Dynasty Six. Unas' and Teti's Pyramid Texts differ slightly from the other corpuses with the inclusion of what has become known as the Cannibal Hymn (Pyramid Text 273/274). This spell is found above the entrance to the serdab in the antechamber in both pyramids; in Unas', it is a complete and unique spell, while in Teti's pyramid, it is shorter.

Teti's mortuary temple is the only portion left of the outer part of the complex, and it conforms almost exactly to those of Djedkare-Isesi and Unas, as do those that follow it.

"THE PERFECTION OF PEPI IS ESTABLISHED," NORTH SAQQARA (PEPI I, DYNASTY SIX)

Pepi I's pyramid is a near-copy of Teti's, with a few minor differences in number and content of Pyramid Texts. It was built of the same materials as that of Teti, and likely with the same stepped inner core. All that remains today, however, is a low mound and a robbers' pit in the middle. It is estimated to have been 172 feet high, and 258 feet on each side. The interior layout of chambers is the same, although Pepi I's was considerably damaged by the removal of any limestone from which to make lime. Most unusually, the pink granite canopic chest was still in situ in front of the sarcophagus, along with a bundle of viscera, presumably the king's.

The mortuary temple is almost completely gone, but enough remains to indicate ground plans almost exactly the same as Djedkare-Isesi's, Unas', and Teti's. The causeway and valley temple have never been excavated.

PYRAMID NAME UNKNOWN, NORTH SAQQARA (MERENRE, DYNASTY SIX)

Merenre ruled for a very short time, and his pyramid was as badly damaged as the previous one in the dynasty. It has never been completely excavated and recorded, although his burial chamber has been cleared. It seems likely that the dimensions were the same as or similar to those of the earlier Sixth Dynasty pyramids.

When the burial chamber was cleared, the sarcophagus was found to contain the body of a young man, with hair braided in the style of Egyptian youths, as a forelock on the right side of the head. It seems unlikely that the body was that of the king, but it remains in the Cairo Museum and has never been studied.

The king seemed to have ruled for such a short time that work simply ceased on his complex when he died. Therefore, very little is left, besides an offering hall and an offering table. There is no sign of a causeway or a valley temple. However, see Document 10 for evidence that it was intended for the pyramid to have a full complement of accoutrements.

"PEPI IS ESTABLISHED AND LIVING," NORTH SAQQARA (PEPI II, DYNASTY SIX)

Pepi II was the last ruler of Dynasty Six, and according to Manetho, he lived for 100 years, ruling for 94 of those. If this is the case, he is the long-ruling king in human history, although it seems unlikely that the numbers are correct. His pyramid was of the usual Dynasty Six size; its base was 258 feet square, and the height was 172 feet. The core was a five-stepped pyramid. It was given retaining walls of small, roughly shaped limestone blocks with a mud mortar. The outer limestone blocks were laid without mortar. The layout and contents of the complex are nearly identical to the earlier Dynasty Six kings, except that the pyramid itself was given what might be described as a retaining wall, 21 feet wide, that ran around the outer edge of the construction. The reasons for this are unclear.

There are scattered fragments of Pepi II's mortuary temple and the reliefs that must have decorated its walls. What is left of the relief indicates that they were very similar to those of Sahure, and it may have been that Pepi II ordered them to be copied into his mortuary temple.

PRIMARY DOCUMENTS

(Translations author's own)

NB: Please note the following conventions used:

. . . – indicates a lacuna or break in the original text

[ ] – indicates restored words or phrases from broken text

< > – indicates restored words or phrases from possible scribal error

( ) – indicates words inserted by translator for added meaning

---

ROYAL DECREES AND INSCRIPTIONS

This section comprises the royal documents that relate directly to pyramids. They are ordered temporally, earliest first. An effort has been made to include all royal texts that are related to the pyramids in any way, thus the inclusions of the triad inscriptions and dedications. The italicized portions found beneath some of the documents' underlined titles are intended to clarify the identity of the speakers, and in the case of the triads, intended to identify the three statues. Document 1 is the only instance that identifies the architect of any pyramid, in this case, the famous Imhotep, about whom we know nothing else. Others are inscriptions from statues from mortuary temples or valley temples, graffiti in the form of dedications left at or on pyramids indicating the worship of the pyramid's owner by later kings who have visited the complexes, and royal decrees concerning the personnel of certain pyramid complexes and their exemptions from taxes and corvée work.

DOCUMENT 1
Inscription on a Statue of Djoser with the Name and Titles of the Architect of the Step Pyramid (Dynasty Three, South Saqqara)

Seal-bearer of Lower Egypt, Royal Chief, Hereditary Nobleman, Governor of the Great Estate, Great Inspector, Imhotep, Carpenter, Sculptor, Carver (?) of All (?).

DOCUMENT 2
Inscriptions on Triads[1] of Menkaure from His Mortuary Temple (Dynasty Four, Giza)

First Triad (Male Figure representing Fourth Upper Egyptian Theban Nome, Menkaure, Hathor)
Words to be spoken (by the nome representation): I have given you everything that is in the south, all provisions(?), and all offerings, because you have risen as the King of Upper and Lower Egypt eternally.

Second Triad (Female Figure representing Seventh Upper Egyptian Diospolitan Nome, Menkaure, Hathor)
Words to be spoken (by the nome representation): I have given you every good thing in it (i.e., the nome), all offerings that are in the south, because you have risen as the King of Upper and Lower Egypt eternally.

*Third Triad (Female Figure representing Kynopolite Nome, Menkaure, Hathor)*Words to be spoken (by the nome representation): I have given you everything good, all offerings, all provisions(?) in the south, eternally.

DOCUMENT 3
Decree of Shepseskaf for the Pyramid of Menkaure (Dynasty Four, Giza)

Horus Shepses-khet: Year after the first occasion of the counting of [all] the cattle and [all] the small animals... Done in the presence of the king himself.

The King of Upper and Lower Egypt Shepseskaf makes as his monument for the King of Upper and Lower Egypt Menkaure a *pekher*-offering[2] ... in the pyramid "Menkaure is Divine" ...

DOCUMENT 4
Inscription from the Mortuary Temple of Sahure
(Dynasty Five, Abusir)

Speech of the Gods to the King
Words to be spoken: I have given you all the statues (lit. likenesses?) together with all provisions that are in all the foreign lands together with every good thing of my possessions.

Words to be spoken: I have given you all the western and eastern foreign lands together with all the columns and all the monuments that are in every foreign land.

Words to be spoken: I have given to you life, all dominion, all health, all joy, and all stability. You are at the head of all the living spirits. You have risen upon the Seat of Horus eternally. . . .

DOCUMENT 5
Dedication of Djedkare-Isesi in the Mortuary Temple of
Niuserre (Dynasty Five, Abusir)

Horus Djed-Khau, King of Upper and Lower Egypt, the Two Ladies Djed-Hor, Djedkare. He made these monuments for the King of Upper and Lower Egypt Niuserre. . . .

DOCUMENT 6
Decree of Pepi I for the Pyramid City of Sneferu
(Dynasty Six, reign of Merire, Dahshur)

Horus Meri-tawy. Regnal year 21, month 3 of Proyet (Winter).

The King's order to . . . the Vizier . . . Overseer of Works Meri-Ptah-Merire, Overseer Ikhy-khenet, Overseer of the Palace Attendants of the Great House Weni, Overseer of the Distribution of the Divine Offerings Khenu, Sole Companion Ikhy-em-per-Merire, Overseer of the Administration of the *heri-wedjeb*[3] Meri, Companion and Overseer of the Interpreters from Medja, Yam, Irtjet . . .

The King of Upper and Lower Egypt Sneferu in the (two) pyramids "Sneferu Shines."

His Majesty orders the exemption for those in the pyramid cities from exportation for any work of the King's Houses, (from levy) for any taxes for any administration of the Residence, (from responsibility) for any obligation to work by order of any person, (and from obligation) from corvée work by order of any person for all eternity.

His Majesty orders the exemption for all the palace attendants of these pyramid cities from the launching of any boats by water or by land, upstream or downstream.

His Majesty orders that no one shall allow the plowing of any field belonging to these two pyramid cities as execution of labor for any dependent of any king, any royal descendent, any Companion or magistrate, from the palace attendants of this pyramid city.

His Majesty orders that no one shall allow the plowing of any field of this pyramid city by any peaceable Nubian.

His Majesty orders that no one shall lead away any foreigner in these two pyramid cities, when they have come from their area of land registry, or when they have come by means of any Egyptian or any peaceable Nubian, namely anyone who has been known to them. Neither shall they be spoken against.

His Majesty orders that no one shall use the female children or the food of a *neher*-cow[4] or one that is the property of the *djeha*,[5] while they are taxable in these pyramid cities.

His Majesty orders that no one shall bring over any people in order to work in service of the pyramid, "The Seat of *Ikaw-Her*[6] is Divine" from these pyramid cities.

His Majesty orders that no one shall count (for taxation purposes) the irrigation canals, the ponds, the wells, the water alleyways, or the trees in these pyramid cities.

His Majesty orders that no peaceable Nubian shall leave, who is required to work in these pyramid cities.

His Majesty orders the distribution of any agricultural shares of these pyramid cities corresponding to the distribution regulations of these pyramid cities.

His Majesty orders the supplementing of any palace attendant of these pyramid cities, while the children of all the permanent inhabitants, who have been given from the land registry of these pyramid cities, have been recruited.

Neither any land, nor priestly income, nor property shall be given to any person who is a resident in any other pyramid city.

Neither shall one give the title of any palace attendant of these pyramid cities to any other person, except in the case of those who were so ordered.

His Majesty has done this for the protection of these pyramid cities from these concerns, so that the priestly service, the monthly offerings, and the divine offerings will be carried out in these pyramid cities [for] the King of Upper and Lower Egypt Sneferu in (both) of the pyramids "Sneferu Shines" by order of the King of Upper and [Lower Egypt, Merire], may he have life, prosperity, and health, may he live [forever].

Sealed in the presence of the King.

DOCUMENT 7
Inscription fragment from the Mortuary Temple of Menkaure (Dynasty Six, reign of Merenre, Giza)

[Horus Ankh-hau]

... [priest] in order to perform the cult in your tomb enclosure and your shrine. . . . [lector priest] in order to read the writing of the art of the lector priest to you. . . . set the name of the King of Upper and Lower Egypt Menkaure on this pyramidion in stone masonry . . .

Sealed in the presence of the King. . . .

DOCUMENT 8
Decree of Pepi II from the Mortuary Temple of Menkaure (Dynasty Six, Giza)

Horus . Regnal year 31, month 4 of Akhet (Inundation), day 6.

The king orders the Overseer of the pyramid city "Menkaure is Divine" . . .

The Hereditary Noble, the eldest son of the king Inti-em-saf, 1 copy. The mayor, Sole Companion, venerated Pepi-Iam, 1 copy. The mayor, Sole Companion, Overseer of the Palace Attendants of the Great House Khnum-hotep, 1 copy.

The lector priest, scribe of the phyle, Ishefy is the Overseer of the pyramid city. . . . No one has a legal claim against it except this Ishefy, in accordance with the instruction . . . forever.

The right of disposal shall not be given to the municipal authorities that any people or any soldiers are caused to go out because of this instruction for . . . the pyramid "Neferkare (Pepi II) is Established and Living" and the pyramid "The Beauty of Merenre Shines," concerning anything to be taken from this pyramid city.

His Majesty orders the exemption and the protection of this pyramid city, so that no one shall take . . . any people to this work because of the priests' services, the monthly services, and the keepers of the divine contract . . . Neferkare, may he live forever, by order of the King of Upper and Lower Egypt Neferkare, may he live for ever and ever.

Sealed in the presence of the King.

DOCUMENT 9
Decree of a Successor of Pepi II for the Cult of the Queens Meri-ankh-nes and Neith (Dynasty Six, South Saqqara)

Horus . . . may he live forever. Year of the Uniting of the Two Lands, month 4 of Shomu (Summer), day 1.

. . .

His Majesty orders the exempting and the protection of the "gods" servants' and the funerary priests, the houses and male children, fields and storehouses as well as the "beloved"[7] people of the King's Mother[8] Meri-ankh-nes, the elder, and the King's Mother Neith from the execution of any corvée work or taxes so that they may carry out the priestly service, the monthly feasts, and the presenting of the divine offerings in the shrines of these two King's Mothers (i.e., Meri-ankh-nes and Neith) for all eternity by order of the King of Upper and Lower Egypt . . . may he live forever and ever.

Sealed in the presence of the King.

NONROYAL AUTOBIOGRAPHY

DOCUMENT 10
Autobiography of Weni, the Elder (Dynasty Six, Abydos)

This autobiography, one of several from the Sixth Dynasty of the Old King-dom, refers to a revolt originating in the harem. The fact that the instigator of the revolt appears to be the First Wife or Queen is extremely important. This kind of document is generally the only provider of such information, without which the history of ancient Egypt would be that much poorer. Weni served under three successive kings, Teti, Merenre, and Pepi I, and he makes much of the fact that he was trusted by all three, and given responsibilities far beyond his rather lowly ranks. Only the sections dealing specifically with the royal house and the procuring of materials for building funerary enclosures and their furnishings have been included, although the entire text is fascinating.

Count, Overseer of the South, Councillor, Guardian of Nekhen, Chief of Nekheb, Sole Companion, Venerated before Osiris Foremost of the Westerners, Weni says:

Weni's work under Teti, second king of the Sixth Dynasty.
I was a young man who tied on the fillet[9] during the reign of the Majesty of Teti, my rank being Overseer of the Storehouse. When I served as Inspector of the Palace Attendants and . . . of the robing room of the Majesty of Pepi (I). His Majesty placed me in the rank of Companion, and Inspector of the "god's servant" of his pyramid city, although my office was (only) . . . His Majesty placed me as Senior Warden of Nekhen. His heart was more filled with me than with any other of his servants. I heard cases by myself together with the vizier with all secrecy [and traveling?] in the name of the king, of the royal private office, of the Six Great Estates, because the heart of His Majesty was more filled with me than with any other of his officials, any other of his nobles, and any other of his servants.

The king grants Weni's request for a stone sarcophagus.
I requested from the hand of the Majesty of my lord that a sarcophagus of white stone be brought from Tura. His Majesty caused that a God's Sealbearer and a crew of sailors in his charge travel [by boat] to bring this sarcophagus from Tura. It (i.e., the sarcophagus) returned with him in the great cargo-boat of the Residence (i.e., the royal house), together with its lid, a false door, two door-jambs, and an offering table. Never before had the like been done for any other servant, because I was excellent in his Majesty's heart, because I was the root of his Majesty's heart, and because his Majesty's heart was filled with me, although I was (only) the Senior Warden of Nekhen.

Weni rises in the king's estimation.
His Majesty placed me as Sole Companion of the Great House,[10] and Overseer of the Palace Attendants. Four officials of the Overseer of the Palace Attendants who were there were expelled. I acted so that his Majesty praised me, in carrying out escort duty, in preparing the royal road, in working in the capacity of aide. I acted perfectly, so that his Majesty praised me extravagantly for it.

Weni's service to the king regarding the harem conspiracy.
When matters against the queen, whose scepter is great, in the royal private office were to be inquired into in secret, his Majesty caused me to go down to judge them, by myself. No other vizier or official was there, except for me, because I was excellent, because I was the root of his Majesty's heart, and because his Majesty filled his heart with me. I acted as scribe, by myself, with only a Senior Warden of Nekhen, although I was (only) an Overseer of the Palace Attendants. Never had the like been heard concerning a private matter of the royal private office, except for his Majesty's having me judge, because I was more excellent in his Majesty's heart than any other of his officials, more than any other of his nobles, more than any other of his servants.

. . .

Weni's service for Merenre, third king of the Sixth Dynasty, including administering the gathering of corvée workers.
When I was in the Great Estate as nurse and sandal-bearer, the King of Upper and Lower Egypt, Merenre, my lord, may he live forever, placed me as Count and Overseer of the South, south at Elephantine and north at Medjnyt. . . . I acted for him as Overseer of the South satisfactorily, . . . I

carried out all the constructions, twice I counted everything countable for the Residence in this south, and all the service (i.e., corvée) that was due to the Residence in this south on two occasions.

. . .

Weni is put in charge of an expedition to quarry stone for accoutrements for Merenre's pyramid, including the pyramidion.
His Majesty sent me to Ibhat to bring a lord of life (i.e., a sarcophagus), a chest of life (i.e., canopic chest?) and its lid, together with a precious and valuable pyramidion for Kha-Nefer-Merenre,[11] my mistress. His Majesty sent me to Elephantine to bring back a granite false door together with its libation table, granite door-jambs and lintels, and to bring back granite doors, libation tables for the upper chapel of Kha-Nefer-Merenre, my mistress. They headed downstream in my charge for Kha-Nefer-Merenre in six barges, three cargo boats, and three "eight-boats" in a single expedition.

. . .

A typical ending for an Old Kingdom autobiography.
I was one beloved of his father, blessed by his mother, pleasant to his brothers, Count, Overseer of the South, revered by Osiris, Weni.

LITERATURE

DOCUMENT 11
Excerpts from King Khufu and the Magicians

This rather long text is a portion of a longer fictional story from Dynasty Fifteen of the Second Intermediate Period (1650–1550 B.C.E.). It weaves three stories together involving Kings Sneferu and Khufu of the Fourth Dynasty; however, the entire work is missing the beginning, so it may well be longer than three stories. The tales seem to be told by courtiers of the king, the first by a man named Bauefre, and the second and third by a Prince Hardedef.

Khufu and the Magician Djadjaemankh
The first tale relates a story within a story, an event that occurred in the time of Khufu's father, Sneferu, and told to Khufu to entertain him. It involves a pleasure boat filled with largely naked young women who row

back and forth on a lake in front of the king and his retinue. One of the
rowers loses a hair ornament and the magician, Djadjaemankh, folds the
water on top of itself to reveal the hair pendant on the bottom.

. . . Bauefre stood and he said, "May I cause that your Majesty hear of the marvels that happened in the time of your father, Sneferu, true of voice, and hear of the actions of the chief lector priest? . . . [There occurred one of those rare days in which the king was restless, and everyone in the royal palace] was looking for some kind of recreation for him, but they could not find it. Then he (the king) said, "Go, bring me the chief lector priest, Djadjaemankh."

He was brought to the king immediately. Then his Majesty said to him, "I have gone around every room of the king's palace, may he live, prosper and be healthy (l.p.h.), seeking recreation for myself, but I cannot find it."

So Djadjaemankh said to him, "Would your majesty please go to the lake of the Great House, (l.p.h.?) Equip a galley with all the beautiful women of the interior of your palace. The heart of your Majesty will be refreshed at seeing them row upstream and downstream, seeing the beautiful marshes of your lake, and seeing its marshlands, its beautiful banks. Indeed, your heart will be refreshed."

"I shall do so," said the king. "Bring me twenty wooden oars worked in gold with wooden grips worked in fine gold. Bring me twenty beautifully shaped women, with deep bosoms and braided hair who have not yet given birth, and bring me twenty nets. Give these nets to the women and set aside their clothes."

So it was done according to all the commands of his Majesty. The women were rowing downstream and upstream (before the royal dais and all the royal court) and the heart of his Majesty was happy, seeing them. Then, one who was at the stroke-oar became entangled in her braid and a fish-shaped pendant of new turquoise fell into the water. She stopped rowing, sitting still, and her side stopped rowing, as well. His Majesty said, "Can't you row?" and they said, "Our stroke-oar has stopped rowing." Then his Majesty said to her, "Why don't you row?" She said, "My fish-shaped pendant has fallen into the water." His Majesty offered to replace the pendant, but she said, "I love my own possession, more than I would a copy of it." His Majesty said, "Bring me the chief lector priest, Djadjaemankh" and he was brought to the king immediately. His Majesty said, "Djadjaemankh, my brother. I have done as you said and indeed, my heart was refreshed to see their rowing. Then a fish-shaped pendant of one of the women fell in the water and she stopped rowing. As a result, she ended up ruining the rhythm of her side. I asked her why she had stopped rowing and she told me about the pendant. I offered to replace it but she refused." Then the chief lector priest Djadjaemankh spoke with magic words, and he folded one half of the lake over the other half. He found the pendant, lying on a turtle shell. He took it up and gave it to its mistress.

Now, the water, which had been 12 cubits[12] deep, was now 24 cubits deep when it had been folded over, so Djadjaemankh spoke with magic words again, and he brought the lake back to its proper position. His Majesty spent the rest of the day holidaying together with the entire palace. And so it turned out that his Majesty rewarded the chief lector priest Djadjaemankh with every good thing. "Look, this wonder happened during the rule of your father, the King of Upper and Lower Egypt, Sneferu, true of voice, and was one of the things the chief lector priest and book-scribe, Djadjaemankh did."

Then the Majesty of the King of Upper and Lower Egypt Khufu, true of voice, said, "Give an offering of one thousand loaves of bread and one hundred jars of beer, one ox, and two incense balls to the Majesty of the King of Upper and Lower Egypt Sneferu, true of voice, and give one cake, one jar of beer and one incense ball to the chief lector priest and book-scribe, Djadjaemankh. I have seen his display of skill." Then all the commands of his Majesty were enacted.

Khufu and the Magician Djedi
> *The second and third stories are told in "real" time, and are tales of magic and myth. The second story seems to be the origin of the terrible reputation of Khufu in later periods, although it is not a reputation that has as yet been verified archaeologically. In asking the magician, Djedi, to cut off the head of a human being in order to replace it, Khufu is flying in the face of the strictures of the gods, apparent evidence of his selfish and brutal nature.*

Then Prince Hardedef stood to speak . . .

" . . . of the knowledge of those who have passed by. It is impossible to tell truth from falsehood. . . ." Then his Majesty said, "What is it, Hardedef, my son?" And Prince Hardedef said, "There is a poor man, whose name is Djedi. He lives in Djed-Sneferu-True-of-Voice. He is a commoner of one hundred and ten years of age. He has eaten five hundred loaves of bread and a side of beef as well as having drunk one hundred jars of beer until today. He knows how to rejoin a head that has been cut off. He knows how to make a lion walk behind him with its leash upon the ground. He knows the number of private offices in the sanctuary of Thoth." The Majesty of the King of Upper and Lower Egypt, Khufu, true of voice, had himself spent much time seeking for those harims of the sanctuary of Thoth, to make a replica for his own tomb. So his Majesty said, "You, Hardedef, my son, you will bring him to me."

Ships were made ready for Prince Hardedef, and he traveled upstream to Djed-Sneferu-True-of-Voice. After the ships were moored at the bank, he traveled by land, sitting in a palanquin of ebony with carrying poles of a costly wood that were mounted in gold. After he reached Djedi, the palanquin was set down and Hardedef stood to address the commoner. He found him lying on a mat in the threshold of his house. A servant was beside him, anointing him, and another was rubbing his feet. Prince Hardedef said, "Your condition is like one who lives in the face of old age, old age being the place of mooring, the place of being buried, the place of joining the earth, as one who sleeps until dawn, devoid of disease, without a hacking cough. Thus, greetings to a venerable one. I have come here to summon you by the behest of my father, Khufu, true of voice. You will eat dainties that the king will give you, like the provisions of those who are in his court. He will conduct you in due time to your forefathers who are in the necropolis." Then Djedi said, "In peace, in peace, Hardedef, prince beloved of his father. May your father, Khufu, true of voice, praise you. May he promote your place among the old men. May your spirit vent anger on your enemy. May your soul know the roads that lead to the portal of hidden sight. Thus, greetings, O Prince." Prince Hardedef extended his arms to Djedi, raising him up. He went with him to the bank, supporting him with his arm. Then Djedi said, "Bring me a traveling barge. It will bring my children and my writings with me." So Hardedef produced two traveling barges with their crews.

Djedi came downstream in the same barge as Prince Hardedef, and after he arrived at the Residence, Prince Hardedef went to report their arrival to the Majesty of the King of Upper and Lower Egypt, Khufu, true of voice. Prince Hardedef said, "O, sovereign, l.p.h., my lord. I have brought Djedi." His Majesty said, "Go and bring him to me." His Majesty proceeded to the columned forecourt of the Great House, and Djedi was ushered into him. His Majesty said, "Why is it that I have not seen you before, Djedi?" and Djedi answered, "The one who comes is the one who is summoned, O sovereign, l.p.h. Summon me, and behold, I come." His Majesty said, "Is the story true that you know how to rejoin a head which has been cut off?" Djedi said, "Yes, I know how to do this, sovereign, l.p.h., my lord." His Majesty said, "Let a prisoner be brought to me and execute his death sentence." Djedi protested, "But not to people, sovereign, l.p.h., my lord. It is forbidden to do such a thing to the noble herd."[13] So a goose was brought to him, its head having been cut off. The body of the goose was put to the west side of the columned forecourt, and its head was put to the eastern side. Djedi spoke words of magic and the goose was standing, waddling, and its head was waddling, too. After the two pieces of goose met, the newly whole goose stood, cackling. Djedi asked for another edible bird to be brought to him, and he treated it as he had treated the goose. Then his Majesty caused a cow to be brought to him, its head cut off and lying on the ground. Djedi again spoke words of magic and the cow was standing, rejoined, behind him with its lead fallen to the ground.

Khufu and the Birth of the Three Royal Children

The third story is the most important of the three, presenting a myth concerning the successors of Khufu. It also presents further evidence of Khufu's bad character, when he feels great sadness at the news of these offspring who are born to a poor couple, and, in the story at any rate, are not of Khufu's royal lineage.

Then the king, Khufu, true of voice, said, "Indeed, is it true that you know the number of the private offices of the sanctuary of Thoth?" Djedi said, "May it please you, I don't know their number, sovereign, l.p.h., my lord, but I do know the place in which the number is." His Majesty said, "Indeed? Where?" Djedi answered, "There is a chest made of flint in the room called Investigation in Heliopolis. It is in that chest. But, sovereign, l.p.h., my lord, I will not be bringing it to you." His Majesty said, "Then who will bring it to me?" Djedi said, "It will be the eldest of three children who are in the belly of Radjedet who will bring it to you." His Majesty said, "I really would like this. About what you've said, who is this Radjedet?" Djedi answered, "She is the wife of a priest of Re, lord of Sakhbu. She is pregnant with three children of Re, lord of Sakhbu.

They will enter this most potent of offices in the entire land, the kingship. The eldest among them will act as the Greatest of Seers in Heliopolis." The heart of his Majesty fell in sadness at this news. Djedi said, "What is this mood, sovereign, l.p.h., my lord? Is it because of the account of these three children? What I said was, 'First your son, then his son, then one of hers." His Majesty said, "When is she going to be giving birth, this Radjedet?" and Djedi answered, "She will give birth in the first month of Proyet on day fifteen." His Majesty said, "That is when the sandbanks of the Two-Fish Channel are cut off. Servant, I will cross to the place myself so that I might see the temple of Re, lord of Sakhbu." Djedi said, "Then I shall cause four cubits of water to occur on the sandbanks of the Two-Fish Channel." His Majesty went to the palace. He said, "Command Djedi to enter into the house of Prince Hardedef so that he will live with him. Make his provisions as a thousand loaves of bread, one hundred jars of beer, one bull, and one hundred bundles of leeks." The commands of his majesty were done.

One day, Radjedet was suffering in herself, and her bearing was painful. The Majesty of Re, lord of Sakhbu said to Isis, Nephthys, Meskhenet, Kheket, and Khnum, "Please go and deliver Radjedet of the three children who are in her belly, who will become kings in this land. They will build your temples. They will endow your altars. They will richly provide your offering tables. They will increase your divine offerings." The goddesses set out, having made their forms as female musicians, Khnum with them as a porter. They arrived at the house of Userre, and they found him standing with his loincloth upside down. They brought him their necklaces and sistra. He said to them, "My ladies, there is a woman who is suffering in herself, her bearing painful." They replied, "Let us see her. Look, we know how to bring about birth." He said, "Proceed, then." They entered the presence of Radjedet and they closed the door of the room. Isis placed herself in front of Radjedet, with Nephthys behind her, while Kheket was hastening the births. Isis said, "May you not be strong in her belly, in your name of 'Strong.'" A child rushed forth into her hands, a child of one cubit, strong of bones, his limbs covered in gold and his royal head-cloth in real lapis-lazuli. They washed him, cutting his umbilical cord, which was then placed on a couch of brick. Then Meskhenet took herself to him and said of him, "The king who will exercise the kingship throughout this whole land." Khnum made his body healthy. Once again, Isis placed herself in front of Radjedet, Nephthys behind her, while Kheket was hastening the births. Isis said, "May you not kick in her belly, in your name of 'Re-who-kicks.'" Another child rushed forth into her arms as a child, one cubit long, strong of bones, his limbs covered in gold, his royal head-cloth in real lapis-lazuli. They washed him, cutting his umbilical cord, which was then placed on a couch of brick. Then Meskhenet took herself to him, and said of him, "The king who will exercise the kingship throughout this whole land." Then Khnum made his body healthy. One last time, Isis placed herself in front of Radjedet, Nephthys behind her, while Kheket was hastening the births. Isis said, "May you not be dark in her belly in your name of Darkness." The child rushed forth into her hands as a child of one cubit, strong of bones, his limbs covered in gold, his royal head-cloth in real lapis-lazuli. Meskhenet took herself to him and said of him, "The king who will exercise the kingship throughout this whole land." Then Khnum made his body healthy. They washed him, cutting his umbilical cord, which was then placed on a couch of brick. The deities went out, having delivered Radjedet of the three children. They said, "May you be joyful, Userre. Look, three children are born to you." He said to them, "My women, what can I do for you? Please take this barley and give it to your porter, and take it for yourselves for payment in beer." Khnum loaded himself with the barley and they went back to the place from which they had come.

Isis said, "What is the reason we came, without performing marvels for the children? Just so that we would report it to their father who asked us to come?" So they made three royal crowns, and they placed them in the barley. Then they caused the sky to fill with wind and rain. They entered the house and said, "Please place the barley here in a sealed room until we return from performing in the north." And so they put the barley in a sealed room. Then Radjedet purified herself in a cleansing ceremony that took fourteen days. She asked her maidservant, "Is the house ready?" And the maidservant replied, "It has been made ready with every good thing, except beer-jars; they have not been brought." Radjedet said, "Indeed why haven't the jars been brought?" And the maidservant said, "There is nothing here that works except the barley of those female musicians. It is in the room that has their seal on it." Radjedet said, "Go and bring barley from it. Userre will give them compensation from it after he comes." The maidservant went, opening the room, and as she did, she heard the sound of praising, singing, dancing, and shouting—everything that is done for a king—in the room. She went and reported everything she'd heard to Radjedet. When Radjedet went into the room, she couldn't find the place from which the noise was made. Finally, she placed her ear to the sack and found that the noise was coming from it. She placed the sack in a box, which was placed inside another, which was sealed and bound with leather. She put it into a room that was full of her belongings, and put a seal on it. When Userre returned from the fields, Radjedet reported the matter to him, and his heart was happier than anything. They spent a happy day.

. . .

It is finished.

PYRAMID TEXTS[14]

DOCUMENT 12
Utterance 467

Utterance 467 is an Utterance concerned with the ascending of the king to the sky and eventually into the divine barque of Re as it sails across the sky carrying the sun. It is a particularly evocative Utterance, and compares the king with Re in a fashion typical of this type of religious text.

. . . Here is the king, Re. This king is your son. The king is a soul. The king is honored. The king is strong, useful of arms, and wide of stride. The king shines in the east like Re. He sails in the west like Kheprer. The king lives by means of that which Horus, lord of the sky, lives, by order of Horus, lord of the sky. The king is pure, Re. The king sits on his seat, the king takes his oar and the king rows Re, traversing the sky [as] a star of gold, a flash of the bull of the sunshine, a spear of gold for he who traverses the sky.

The flier flies up. The king flies up from you, O humans. He is not of the land. He is of the sky. O local god, the spirit of the king is beside you. He has soared to the sky as a heron. He has kissed the sky as a falcon. He has reached the sky as a locust that belongs to the sun. The king has not opposed the (new) king. He has not helped Bastet. The king has not danced as the great one of the carrying chair. Does a son of Re make his place? Then he makes the place of the king. Is the son of Re healthy? Then the king will be healthy. Is he hungry? Then the king is hungry....

DOCUMENT 13
Utterance 477

Utterance 477 is one of only two pieces of narrative myth in the Pyramid Texts, the other being Utterance 527, below. This Utterance provides a glimpse into the trial of Seth, for the murder of his brother, Osiris. This event led to the installation of Osiris as the deity responsible for the dead and for the West that the dead inhabited, and it led to the fight between Horus, the son of Osiris, and Seth for the throne of Egypt. Thus, the Utterance ultimately concerns the unification of Egypt, with a divine justification.

Words to be spoken: The sky reels, and the land trembles. Horus comes, and Thoth appears. They raise Osiris upon his side, and they help him to stand up before the Two Enneads. Remember, Seth, and place in your heart this speech that Geb said, this threat that the gods made against you in the Estate of the Elder in Heliopolis, because you threw Osiris to the ground, when you, Seth, said, "I did not do this against him," so that you might have power therefrom, you having been rescued, so that you might have power over Horus; when you, Seth, said, "He was the one who attacked me," and this his name of One-who-attacks-the-earth came into being; when you, Seth, said, "He is the one who kicked me," and this his name of Orion came into being, long of leg and wide of stride, who is pre-eminent in Upper Egypt....

DOCUMENT 14
Utterance 507

This Utterance gives some idea of the geography of the afterlife in the sky. Several canals are mentioned, about which nothing is known, other than their names in ancient Egyptian, as well as the Field of Rushes. The fact that landing places are necessary for the king to land attests to the watery nature of the sky, and incidentally, to the importance water, particularly rivers and marshes, held in the ancient Egyptian world view. This Utterance also contains indications of the origins of the moon and the stars, as well as various inhabitants of the sky.

Words to be spoken: O *Ikhemty*.[15] Say to he who has, "He who has not is here." The *Ban*-canal is open. The Field of Rushes is flooded. The *Kha*-canal is full of water. The two landing places are set in the sky for Horus, so that he may cross over them to Re. The two landing places are set in the sky for Re, so that he might cross over them to Re-Harakhti. He commends the king to his father, the moon. The offspring of the king are the morning stars. He commends the king to the four children who sit upon the eastern side of the sky. He commends the king to the four children who sit upon the western side of the sky, and to the four children whose hair is coal-black, who sit under the sunshade of the sanctuary tower of *Kheti*. Words to be spoken: The king's father is great. The king's father is great. The king will be as a "father-is-great."

DOCUMENT 15
Utterance 527

Together with Utterance 477, Utterance 527 represents the two earliest narrative myths found in Egyptian literature. As a cosmogonic myth laying out the origins of the universe, it is of particular importance, and is the beginning of the divine Ennead, or group of nine original and primordial deities.

Words to be spoken: Atum is the one who came into being, who masturbated in Heliopolis. He took his phallus in his grasp, so that he might create an orgasm with it. So the twins, Shu and Tefnut were born. They have placed the king between them, and they have placed the king among the gods at the beginning of the Field of Offerings. Words to be spoken four times: May the king go up to the sky, may the king go down to the earth.

DOCUMENT 16
Utterance 650

Utterance 650 places the king firmly in the family of the pantheon and establishes his divine antecedents. Incidentally, it also provides the living king with divine ancestors, emphasizing the connection between the earthly throne and the pantheon.

... This king is Osiris, whom Nut bore. She has caused him to rise in glory as King of Upper and Lower Egypt, in all his dignity.... Anubis, Foremost of the Westerners, Osiris the son of Geb ... the gods and Andjety who is at the head of the eastern nomes. The one who produced the land is the king, so that he might exist at the head of the gods of the sky, like Geb who is at the forefront of the Ennead. His mother the sky bears him, alive, every day like the sun. He appears with him in the east and he sets with him in the west. His mother, Nut, is not free from him on any day. His son provides this king with life. He makes him joyful. He makes him happy. He establishes Upper Egypt for him and establishes Lower Egypt for him. He destroys the fortresses of Asia for him. He throws off the rebellious subjects under his fingers.

DOCUMENT 17
Utterance 723

As can be seen in the following Utterance, the corpse was extremely important to the dead king. Again, it emphasizes the connection between the king and the deities by noting that the king's corpse belongs to a god. In other words, as king is a god, the corpse being his. This Utterance is also found in the funerary text corpus known as the Coffin Texts, as Coffin Text 219.

Words to be spoken: O king, raise yourself upon your bones of iron and your limbs of gold, because this body of yours, it belongs to a god. It cannot grow moldy, it cannot perish, it cannot putrefy. Your mouth is warm. The breath that enters it is from the nostrils of Seth. The winds of the sky perish if the warmth in your mouth perishes. The sky will be bereft of its stars if the warmth that is in your mouth is taken away. Your flesh will be born to life. Your life will be more than the life of the stars when they live.

NOTES

1. Triads are sculptural groups of three figures.
2. Perhaps an offering for the king in his transitory state of being.
3. *Heri-wedjeb* is a governmental title, literally translated as "The one who is in charge of the reversion?" Regarding its attendant duties, nothing is known.
4. A *neher* is a type of horned cow, judging from the hieroglyphs. More concerning its species is not known.
5. *Djeha* is a noun having something to do with taxes (perhaps "those taxed"?). No further translation is possible.
6. *Ikaw-Her* seems to be an epithet of the god, Horus, although the word *ikaw* is untranslatable.

7. This may indicate the members of the queen's staff closest in her affection, or it may be a reference to the funerary singers of the queen.

8. A King's Mother was the mother of the king on the throne, rather like the Queen Mother was in the British royal family. In this case, Meri-ankh-nes was the mother of Pepi II, and Neith was his chief queen, although whether it was her son who took over the throne upon the death of Pepi II and the short-lived queen, Nitokret, who followed him, is unknown.

9. Tying on the fillet seems to have been a rite of passage into adulthood and work in the government.

10. Sole Companion of the Great House is an epithet (as opposed to a title, which carries governmental duties with it) given to nearly every courtier in the king's court. Epithets were given as indications of relative closeness to the throne and the king. As an epithet that was virtually ubiquitous, "Sole Companion" is considered by modern scholars to have been an entry-level kind of label, and did not indicate a particularly close or exclusive relationship with the king.

11. Merenre's pyramid.

12. One cubit is the length from the tip of the middle finger to the tip of the elbow.

13. Humans were called "the cattle of the gods" in the religious literature.

14. The Utterance numbers of the Pyramid Texts presented here are those from the hieroglyphic texts arranged by Kurt Sethe and from Raymond Faulkner's translations. James Allen's translation uses different numbers for each pyramid, as he organizes the texts according to each pyramid, rather than collating them.

15. Unknown deity.

GLOSSARY

B.C.E.: Before Common Era: historically neutral way of referring to dating equivalent to Western calendar designation of B.C.

canopic chest, canopic jars: a chest with four accompanying jars, often made from alabaster for the viscera of the deceased. The heads of the jars were shaped as the heads of the four sons of Horus, Imsety, Duamutef, Hapy, and Qebesenuef. The jar with Imsety's head, which was human, held the liver; Duamutef's, with a jackal head, contained the stomach; Hapy's, a baboon head, held the lungs; and Qebesenuef, with a falcon's head, held the intestines. These were kept for the king in the afterlife, so that he would have all necessary parts of his body therein.

cataract: the cataracts in the Nile River, of which there are five, are portions of the river that are blocked or made difficult for passage by naturally occurring, very large limestone boulders. In ancient times from the Old Kingdom until the New Kingdom, the Egyptians maintained a series of fortresses at the cataracts to protect against incursions from the south, as well as to monitor traffic in the surrounding deserts. The First Cataract was, for all intents and purposes, the lower boundary of Egyptian rule, although it was by no means the lower boundary of Egyptian influence.

clerestory lighting: a row of windows, in churches and railway carriages, for example, that sit just below the ceiling; these, together with holes in the ceiling, were often the only natural lighting in Egyptian temples.

corbelled ceilings: an architectural practice of creating a ceiling by bringing the stone blocks used in construction consecutively closer toward each other, every block overhanging the next lower block, until they are close enough to be spanned by a single large block of stone; this creates a vaulted ceiling, and very strong engineering element.

corvée: a system of labor in which citizens of a country or an estate are required to give a certain amount of time in work to the ruler of the country or owner of the estate; likely the system used to build the pyramids.

cosmogony: a myth that explains the origins of the universe; also known as "creation myths."

cult, cultic activity: the religious rituals and practices relating to a particular deity or king.

duat: the "heaven" of ancient Egyptian religion; exactly where the *duat* is located is still debated; however, it seems to include most of the geographical and topographical features of an earthly Egypt; it is peopled by different entities in different periods in Egyptian history.

ennead: a group of nine things; in the context of Egyptian religion, it refers to a group of nine gods, specifically the Heliopolitan Ennead of Atum, Shu, Tefnut, Geb, Nut, Osiris, Isis, Seth, and Nephthys.

gnomon: a device such as a pole that is used in the telling of time or direction by measuring the shadow it casts; a common type of gnomon is the triangle used in the middle of sundials.

in situ: in the original place.

ivory labels: small rectangular pieces of ivory used anciently to identify various products, most often wine, in jars; the tags were inscribed with the identification of the product, and the name and regnal year of the king during which the product was made.

mastaba: from the Arabic word for the benches found outside houses in the countryside in modern Upper Egypt; the superstructure of a tomb, generally belonging to a wealthy and/or noble Egyptian. Built of mudbrick or stone with a rubble (or other) interior and usually rectangular, mastabas could be small or very large; they were built in the style of a bench, and were solid inside, with the exception of tomb shafts and the accompanying tomb chambers. Later in the Old Kingdom, mastabas had attached chapels where offerings could be laid and prayers spoken for the deceased.

obelisk: a tall and narrow stone monument, usually made out of one piece of stone, square with a tapering, shaped point at the top; one of the most famous of these is the obelisk known erroneously as Cleopatra's Needle in Paris (it was made originally for Queen Hatshepsut of the Eighteenth Dynasty), another is the Washington Monument, in the National Mall in front of the White House in Washington, DC.

ogdoad: a group of eight things; in the context of Egyptian religion, it refers to a group of eight gods, specifically the Hermopolitan Ogdoad of Amun, Amunet, Kek, Keket, Heh, Hehet, Nun, and Nunet

ostraca: see potsherds (or sherds)

Palermo Stone: a list of kings carved onto a stela of black basalt, now in the Palermo Archaeological Museum, Sicily, which lists kings of Lower Egypt from mythological beginnings of Egypt's history to the Fifth Dynasty. The texts are listed as a number of horizontal registers, divided into blocks by a vertical line that curves at the top, perhaps as the hieroglyphic sign for the word "year"; each block is for a separate king and indicates the memorable events during each king's reign. The dates on the stone refer, apparently, to the number of biennial cattle counts rather than to the actual years of a king's reign; types of events that are described include religious ceremonies, trade expeditions and their produce, wars, sculpture, and buildings.

pantheon: a group or community of deities, in the case of Egypt, numbering hundreds of gods and goddesses. Some of the most important members of the Egyptian pantheon include Re (sun god), Osiris (god of the underworld and the dead; brother and husband of Isis), Isis (goddess of cosmic associations; wife and sister of Osiris), Horus (god of the throne and the institution of kingship; son of Osiris and Isis), Seth (god of discord, storm, and trickery; brother of Osiris and Isis), Atum (primeval god; "the finished or complete one"), Amun ("the hidden one"; state god of the Eighteenth Dynasty; one of the primeval eight deities who were around before the earth), Thoth (god of knowledge and writing).

phyles: a group or gang of workmen; Old Kingdom temples and pyramids had phyles of workmen to build the pyramids and temples, and to perform the necessary diurnal and nocturnal rituals within the temples, as priests.

polytheism: worshipping more than one god.

potsherds (or sherds): pieces of broken pottery; often these were used as a cheap and plentiful source of medium on which to write, and when written on, they are known as ostraca; when inscribed with the names of kings, they are a very important source of information for trade and forays into surrounding lands.

Pyramid Texts: the oldest corpus of religious texts in the world, written on the walls of the entrance corridors, antechambers, and funerary chambers of the pyramids of the last king of the Fifth Dynasty, Unas, and all the kings of the Sixth Dynasty, and one ruler of the Seventh and Eighth Dynasties, as well as three pyramids belonging to queens of the last king of the Sixth Dynasty, Pepi II. They were intended to aid in the ascent of the king (or queen) into the afterlife in the sky.

register: in art, scenes separated by a ground line, generally in Egyptian art occurring on top of each other; the ground lines are meant to indicate the earth or some floor upon which the figures stand; although the registers appear in vertical order, often the observer is meant to understand them as occurring one behind the other.

sarcophagus: a coffin made of wood or stone or, in the case of the Twenty-Sixth Dynasty, silver usually in a mummiform-shape; the sarcophagus was known, in ancient Egyptian, as the "possessor of life"; royal burials generally had more than one sarcophagus, each nested within the next; they were generally richly decorated and often were partially or wholly covered with gold or silver leaf.

Sed **Festival:** the king's jubilee festival, usually celebrated after the thirtieth year of rule. This festival involved a number of rites, including one that required the king to run around an area demarcated by two B-shaped stone markers; the most famous of the buildings erected to accompany the festival are found in the courtyard of Djoser's Step Pyramid; the festival seems to have been intended as a rejuvenation of the king, as well perhaps as an indication of the king's physical fitness to rule. In Egyptian, *heb sed.*

serdab: from the Arabic, meaning "cellar," or "enclosed niche": a small room attached to mastabas, including the Step Pyramid, also known as a statue chamber, with openings in the walls through which statues of the owner of the mastaba could "look."

serekh: a representation of a palace façade within which the names of the earliest kings of Egypt were written and on top of which a Horus falcon, or occasionally a Seth-animal, perched.

sistrum, sistra (pl.): a rattle usually associated with Hathor, consisting of two flat metal pieces with three narrow metal rods strung between them, and a handle; usually, the top of the handle, attached to the rattle, was in the form of Hathor's head; known throughout Egypt's history.

syncretism: as applied to Egyptian religion only, this involves the joining of two deities to become one; for example, the uniting of Amun and Re to create Amun-Re, the foremost deity of the New Kingdom.

theophoric name: a name that includes a deity's name within it; for example, Menkaure (Men-kau-Re) of the Fourth Dynasty, meaning

"Established are the souls of Re"; nearly every Egyptian name was theophoric, common as well as royal.

titulary: a word peculiar to Egyptological studies meaning the five royal names. The first name is the Horus name, is the oldest, and is written with a falcon on top of a *serekh* within which was written the king's name. The second name is the Two Ladies' name from Dynasty One, the Two Ladies being Nekhbet, the vulture-goddess of Upper Egypt, and Wadjet, the cobra-goddess of Lower Egypt. The third name is the Horus of Gold name, from Dynasty Four. The fourth and fifth names are known as the *nesu-bity* or King of Upper Egypt (*nesu*) and the King of Lower Egypt (*bity*), are the king's throne names, and are always written enclosed in cartouches; the fourth name, *nesu*, is known as the prenomen, and the fifth, *bity*, is the nomen, also known as the Son of Re name.

tumulus: a mound covering an archaeological site, particularly a grave, but also town sites.

Turin Canon: papyrus with list of kings, dated from the Ramesside period (the late New Kingdom) approximately 1400 B.C.E. It begins with a list of kings from a mythological time during which Egypt was ruled by deities and goes to the end of the Second Intermediate Period, listing the rulers with fair accuracy. However, despite the fact that it seems to have been compiled with accuracy in mind, the list has been contradicted by archaeological evidence in several instances, among which is the archaeologically erroneous assertion in the Canon that Nebka was the first king of the Third Dynasty.

wadi: from the Arabic word, meaning a dry riverbed leading into the Nile valley from the surrounding Eastern and Western Deserts.

ANNOTATED BIBLIOGRAPHY

BOOKS

Architecture and Archaeology

Arnold, Dieter. *Building Egypt: Pharaonic Stone Masonry*. Oxford: Oxford University Press, 1991. A fascinating study of all facets of stone masonry, with much of the evidence coming from the pyramid-building age.

Brovarski, Edward. *The Senedjemib Complex, Parts 1 & 2: The Mastabas of Senedjemib Inti (G 2370), Khnumenti (G 2374), and Senedjemib Mehi (G 2378)*. Boston, MA: Museum of Fine Arts, 2001. Volumes in the same series as those of Weeks and Roth (below), the introduction and Chapter 2, Architecture and Decoration, of Part 1 are of particular use. The material that follows is extremely valuable, but may be too technical for the casual reader. The second volume is the book of plates.

Butzer, Karl. *Early Hydraulic Civilization in Egypt: A Study in Cultural Ecology*. Chicago: University of Chicago Press, 1976. A good resource for understanding the topography and geology of Egypt, particularly the pyramids.

Clarke, Somers and R. Engelbach, *Ancient Egyptian Construction and Architecture*. New York: Dover Publications, Ltd., 1930. An extremely useful publication, well-illustrated with photographs and drawings by an early Egyptologist, who also trained as an engineer.

Edwards, I.E.S., *The Pyramids of Egypt*, rev. ed. Harmondsworth, UK: Penguin Books, Ltd., 1991. Long the most complete book on the pyramids and still an essential reference. Although some of the information is out-of-date, it is without parallel as a single source for measurements, decoration, and ground plans.

Jenkins, N. *The Boat Beneath the Pyramids: King Cheops' Royal Ship*. London: Thames and Hudson, Ltd., 1980. Although the title is a misnomer (the boat was found beside the pyramid, not beneath it), this is a well-written and useful account of the excavation and reconstruction of Khufu's boat. The photographs are exceptional and would otherwise be unavailable.

Kees, Hermann. *Ancient Egypt: A Cultural Topography.* Translated by Ian Morrow. London: University of Chicago Press, 1961. A study of ancient Egyptian landscape and history from a geographical point of view.

Lehner, Mark. *The Complete Pyramids.* Cairo: American University in Cairo Press, 1997. A particularly useful work written by an archaeologist who has excavated on the Giza plateau for over twenty years, this book provides a comprehensive look at all the pyramids in Egypt, and includes the Meroitic pyramids in the Sudan.

Lucas, A. *Ancient Egyptian Materials and Industries,* 4th ed., rev. and ed. J.R. Harris, London: Histories and Mysteries of Man Ltd., 1989. This reprint of a 1926 publication studies the materials used in all types of Egyptian craftsmanship, from jewelry to architecture.

Nicholson, P.T. and Ian Shaw. *Ancient Egyptian Materials and Technology,* New York: Cambridge University Press, 1999. This is a series of essays on Egyptian materials and their uses. The entire pharaonic period is covered, so care should be used if the Old Kingdom is the focus of research. However, this is an exceptional volume, and should be consulted in any discussion of how Egyptians worked and the materials with which they worked.

Quirke, S., ed. *The Temple in Ancient Egypt.* London: British Museum Press, 1997. This series of articles based on the temple throughout Egyptian history by some of the most important Egyptologists is exceptionally useful for studying pyramid temples and the place of the temple in society.

Roth, A.M. *A Cemetery of Palace Attendants.* Boston, MA: Museum of Fine Arts, 1995. A collation of the art and excavation of a series of mastabas belonging to a group of palace workers on the Giza plateau in the Western Cemetery, it is in the same series as that of Brovarski (above) and Weeks (below). The introduction and following discussion of the material is of great value to understanding the place of the palace attendant in the palace and in the cemetery fields surrounding the pyramids.

Russell, Terence M., ed. *The Napoleonic Survey of Egypt: The Monuments and Customs of Egypt,* 2 vols. Aldershot, UK: Ashgate Publishing Company, 2001. This draws on the numerous firsthand reports of the French exploration and is the first book in Egypt to give an accessible account of the origins of the French expedition.

Shafer, Byron, ed. *Temples of Ancient Egypt.* Ithaca, NY: Cornell University Press, 1997. Five contributions from eminent scholars on the temples, their architecture, and their rituals from all periods in Egypt.

Verner, Miroslav. *The Pyramids*. Translated from German by Steven Rendall. Cairo: American University of Cairo Press, 2002. A highly readable and valuable reference written by a preeminent archaeologist in the field. As director of the Czech excavations at Abusir since the late 1970s, Verner has the most up-to-date information on the newest discoveries.

Ward, Cheryl. *Sacred and Secular: Ancient Egyptian Ships and Boats*. Dubuque, IA: Kendall/Hunt Publishing Co., 2000. A complete discussion of all Egyptian boats, both those used in riverine traffic, and those used in funerary practices.

Weeks, Kent R., *Mastabas of Cemetery G 6000, Including G 6010 (Neferbauptah); G 6020 (Iymery); G 6030 (Ity); G 6040 (Shepseskafankh)*. Boston, MA: Museum of Fine Arts, 1994. This volume, in the same series as that of Brovarski and Roth, above, discusses in detail the tombs of the palace retainers and attendants in the part of the Western Cemetery at Giza known as G 6000. While much of the detail may be too fine for the general reader, the introduction and Part One, Names and Titles in Cemetery G 6000, are very useful and give a good idea of how the architecture and the tomb owners were linked.

Wildung, D. *Egypt: From Prehistoric to the Romans*. Köln: Taschen GmbH, 2004. An overarching study of Egyptian architecture, useful particularly for the chapters on the architecture of early tombs and of the pyramids.

Art

Cwiek, Andrzej. *Relief Decoration in the Royal Funerary Complexes of the Old Kingdom*. Unpublished PhD thesis. Warsaw University, 2003. The only work of its kind and written in English, this is a remarkably useful collation of the decorations in every pyramid of the Old Kingdom that is readily available on the Internet: www.gizapyramids.org/code/emuseum.asp?newpage=authors_list#c.

Museum catalogue. *Egyptian Art in the Age of the Pyramids*. New York: The Metropolitan Museum of Art, 1999. This catalogue produced to go with the exhibition held at the Metropolitan, the Louvre, and the Royal Ontario Museums has exceptional photographs, and contains fifteen essays solely devoted to Old Kingdom art.

Museum catalogue. *Egyptomania*. Ottawa: Publications Division, National Gallery of Canada, 1994. This catalogue, dedicated to the exhibition called Egyptomania that was held in the Louvre, the National Gallery of Canada, and the Kunsthistorisches Museum in Vienna, provides a fascinating look at the effect ancient Egypt has had on the decorative arts.

Museum catalogue. *Mistress of the House, Mistress of Heaven: Women in Ancient Egypt*. New York: Hudson Hills Press, 1996. This catalogue intended to accompany the exhibition in the Cincinnati Art Museum and the Brooklyn Museum of Art covers women throughout Egyptian history, and is useful for the Old Kingdom.

Robins, Gay. *The Art of Ancient Egypt.* Cambridge, MA: Harvard University Press, 1997. A comprehensive, very well-illustrated study of Egyptian art from the earliest period to the latest.

————. *Proportion and Style in Ancient Egyptian Art.* Austin: University of Texas Press, 1994. A thorough and meticulous discussion of the squared grid used throughout Egyptian history that examines the differences between the grids used in the various periods.

Schafer, Heinrich. *Principles of Egyptian Art.* Translated by J. Baines. Oxford: Oxford University Press, 1986. A seminal and somewhat difficult work on art throughout Egyptian history that is nevertheless extremely valuable for an understanding of how Egyptian art works.

Chronologies, Histories, and Landscape

Andreu, Guillemette. *Egypt in the Age of the Pyramids.* Translated by David Lorton, Ithaca, NY: Cornell University Press, 1997. This primarily social, rather than political, history well sets apart the Old and Middle Kingdoms.

Baines, John and Jaromir Malek. *The Atlas of Ancient Egypt,* 2nd ed. Cairo: American University in Cairo Press, 2002 This is a nearly complete listing, in gazetteer format, of the archaeological sites both within and outside Egypt's borders that discusses the remaining architecture and geography at each site. Includes full-color maps.

Clayton, Peter. *Chronicle of the Pharaohs The Reign by Reign Record of the Rulers and Dynasties of Ancient Egypt,* new ed. London: Thames and Hudson Ltd., 2006. A general chronology, vital for any study of ancient Egypt.

Donadoni, S. ed. *The Egyptians.* Chicago: University of Chicago Press, 1997 Eleven essays on various aspects of Egyptian society, including peasants, scribes, bureaucrats, the dead, etc. Gives a very good overview of the hierarchy and place of one's work in ancient Egypt.

Eyre, C. J., "Work and Organisation of Work in the Old Kingdom." In *Labor in the Ancient Near East,* ed. M. Powell. New Haven, CT: American Oriental Society, 1987, 5–47. A very thorough essay on work in the Old Kingdom. This includes quite an important discussion on the organization of work on the Giza Plateau.

Fischer, Henry G. *Egyptian Women of the Old Kingdom and the Heracleopolitan Period,* 2nd ed. New York: The Metropolitan Museum of Art, 2000. Primarily a work concerned with nonroyal women, hence of great value, as most of what we know of women during this period comes from queens, who are not representative of the greater number of Egyptian women.

Kanawati, Naguib. *Conspiracies in the Egyptian Palace: Unis to Pepy I*. London: Routledge, 2002 A fascinating look at the literary and archaeological evidence for conspiracies against the king during the Sixth Dynasty.

Kemp, Barry. *Ancient Egypt: Anatomy of a Civilization*, 2nd ed., London: Routledge, 2006. A landmark study of Egyptian society written from a specifically archaeological perspective.

Malek, Jaromir and W. Forman. *In the Shadow of the Pyramids: Egypt During the Old Kingdom*. London: Orbis, 1986 A good, popular, and accessible history of the Old Kingdom in particular.

Roth, A.M. *Egyptian Phyles in the Old Kingdom: The Evolution of a System of Social Organization*, Chicago: University of Chicago Press, 1991. A study of the gangs of workmen who built the pyramids and who worked in other ventures for the state in the Old Kingdom.

Shaw, I., ed. *The Oxford History of Ancient Egypt*, new ed., Oxford: Oxford University Press, 2003. This easy to read series of essays written by some of the most eminent scholars in the field provides up-to-date information from the new discoveries made each season in excavations throughout Egypt.

Wilkinson, Toby A.H. *Early Dynastic Egypt*. London: Routledge, 1999. This exhaustive and accessible survey of Dynasties One through Three provides a particularly interesting overview of the process of empire building and statehood.

Language and Literature

Adkins, Lesley and Roy. *The Keys of Egypt: The Race to Crack the Hieroglyphic Code*. New York: HarperCollins Publishers, 2001. An engagingly written story about the decipherment of hieroglyphs in 1822 that provides a good overview of the difficulties in deciphering a new language with a previously impenetrable script.

Allen, James P., translator. *The Ancient Egyptian Pyramid Texts*. Atlanta, GA: Society of Biblical Literature, 2005. The latest translation of the Pyramid Texts, compiled according to pyramid and ordered from those in the burial chamber first, moving through the chambers to the entranceways.

Faulkner, R.O., translator. *The Ancient Egyptian Pyramid Texts*. Oxford: Oxford University Press, 1998. A complete translation of the texts found inside the pyramid chambers from the end of the Fifth and all of the Sixth Dynasties.

Forman, W. and S. Quirke, *Hieroglyphs and the Afterlife in Ancient Egypt*. Norman: University of Oklahoma Press, 1996. A general history of the funerary texts, where they are found, and discussions of how they operated. Very well-illustrated and well-written.

Hornung, Erik. *The Ancient Egyptian Books of the Afterlife*. Translated by David Lorton, Ithaca, NY: Cornell University Press, 1999. An introduction to the religious books of the Egyptians, discussed in order of appearance. Good for establishing the role of the Pyramid Texts among the many other funerary books.

Lichtheim, Miriam, translator. *Ancient Egyptian Literature, vol. 1: The Old and Middle Kingdoms*. Berkeley: University of California Press, 1973. This compilation includes translations of didactic literature, royal inscriptions, and religious literature among other genres from the Old Kingdom.

Wente, Edward, translator. *Letters from Ancient Egypt*. Atlanta, GA: Scholars Press, 1990. Translations of Old Kingdom letters including those from the king to courtiers, from viziers to courtiers, etc.

Religion

Assmann, J. *The Search for God in Ancient Egypt*. Translated by David Lorton. Ithaca, NY: Cornell University Press, 2001. By one of the most perceptive writers on Egyptian religion, this is an intense and deep analysis of the complexity of Egyptian religious thought.

Boylan, P. Thoth. *The Hermes of Egypt*. Oxford: Oxford University Press, 1922. A somewhat dated but still very useful look at Thoth, the god of scribes and intelligence. Very good for Thoth's place in the sun barque with Re in the Pyramid Texts.

David, A.R. *The Ancient Egyptians: Religious Beliefs and Practices*. London: Routledge, 1982. A particularly good book for the study of religious practices throughout Egyptian history, not just the Old Kingdom, so one must be vigilant regarding the time periods.

Hart, George. *Egyptian Myths*. London: British Museum Press, 1990. A brief look at the various myths in Egyptian religious literature, with information otherwise sometimes difficult to find in English.

Hornung, E. *Conceptions of God in Ancient Egypt: The One and the Many*. Translated by J. Baines. London: Routledge & Kegan Paul Ltd., 1982. An indispensable study of the character of Egyptian gods, their worship, and Egyptian theology.

Lesko, Barbara. *The Great Goddesses of Egypt*. Norman: University of Oklahoma Press, 1999. A very accessible and informative book written for popular consumption by a well-known Egyptologist whose field of research is women in ancient Egypt.

Meeks, D. and C. Favard-Meeks. *Daily Life of the Egyptian Gods*. Translated by G.M. Goshgarian, Ithaca, NY: Cornell University Press, 1996. An exceptionally good introduction to the world of the deities of ancient Egypt, with a discussion of the king and his place in that world.

Quirke, Stephen. *Ancient Egyptian Religion*. London: British Museum Press, 1992. A basic and comprehensive look at Egyptian religion.

———. *The Cult of Ra: Sun-Worship in Ancient Egypt*. London: Thames and Hudson Ltd., 2001. A discussion of sun-worship especially during the Old Kingdom.

Simpson, W.K., ed. *Religion and Philosophy in Ancient Egypt*. New Haven, CT: Yale Egyptological Seminar, Dept. of Near Eastern Languages and Civilizations, The Graduate School, Yale University, 1989. A collection of essays written on the topics of religion and philosophy. Of particular use are the first one on the cosmology of the Pyramid Texts, and the last one on the aspects of death and initiation in the funerary parts of the religion.

Spencer, A.J. *Death in Ancient Egypt*. Harmondsworth, UK: Penguin Books Ltd., 1982. A somewhat dated but important book that gives a comprehensive and accessible overview of Egypt's perception of death, and how they dealt with it.

Wilkinson, Richard H. *The Complete Gods and Goddesses of Ancient Egypt*. London: Thames and Hudson Ltd., 2003. As the title says, a complete list of all the deities in Egyptian religion.

INTERNET SITES

General

Centre for Egyptological Studies of the Russian Academy of Sciences: http://cesras.ru/eng/. Russian Egyptologists have contributed seminal work to the study of ancient Egypt, but due to language difficulties, most of their work is not known in the West. This site addresses that and provides information on Russian excavations in Egypt.

Desheret: http://www.desheret.org/. Museum and gallery guide. This site lists many of the museums around the world that maintain Egyptological collections, some of which are quite difficult to get to, making the photos of the objects therefrom particularly useful.

Digital Egypt for Universities: http://www.digitalegypt.ucl.ac.uk/. Don't be put off by the "for Universities," this is a wonderful source for illustrations and history.

Discovery of the Tombs of the Builders of the Pyramids: http://guardians.net/ hawass/buildtomb.htm. Written for a tourist Web site by the excavator of the tombs in a very readable and personable style.

Egypt Exploration Society: http://www.ees.ac.uk/home/whatsnew.htm. The Egypt Exploration Society has been in existence almost since the beginning of Egyptology, and members have participated in most of the original excavations in Egypt. Very useful for discussions of ongoing EES excavations.

Egyptology Resources: http://www.newton.cam.ac.uk/egypt/. Contains links to a large number of Internet scholarly sites.

ETANA (Electronic Tools and Ancient Near Eastern Archives): http://www. etana.org/. A site from the University of Chicago's Oriental Institute with a vast array of downloadable books, most of which are out-of-print. Most of these are the site reports of Egyptology's first excavators, which are often the only source of data for those excavations.

Eternal Egypt: http://www.eternalegypt.org/. The official Web site of the Supreme Council of Antiquities of Egypt, the government department responsible for overseeing the care and excavations of all the sites in Egypt.

Giza Archives Project: http://www.gizapyramids.org/code/emuseum.asp/. A collation of the work of the early excavators on the Giza plateau. Exceptionally thorough and very well-illustrated.

Mark Lehner's Giza Page: http://www.aeraweb.org/. The site of the excavator who has been working at Giza for over twenty years.

Pyramid Cam: http://www.pyramidcam.com/. A live Web camera set on top of a hotel overlooking the pyramids, giving an interesting view of the pyramids at all times during the day.

UNESCO World Heritage Site: http://whc.unesco.org. Overall a wonderful site, with the reasons for each choice of heritage site discussed. Egypt has a number of World Heritage Sites, all of which are discussed, with maps and visuals. Very useful in discussions of ancient Egypt in modern society.

INDEX

Abu Roash, 10, 46
  Abusir, 13, 50
  art in Sahure's causeway in, 78
  pyramid field of, 5
  valley temples at, 67
Abydos, 3–4, 8
  funerary enclosures at, 6
  seat of government at, 14
  tombs at, 36, 39, 45
Administration
  departments of, 8
  formation of, 6
  governors of, 60–61
  hierarchical nature of, 61
  hierarchy of, 8
  state administration, 3, 6
  town administration, 61
  women in, 65
Afghanistan, 7
Afterlife, 17, 23
  royal landscape of, 43
  world of gods, 19
Alexander the Great, 81
Alexandria, 86
Anatolia, 7
Arabia, 7
Archaic Period. See Early Dynastic
    Period

Architecture
  progression in, 4
  of valley temples, 68
Artistic canon, 74
  types of schemes in, 76
  used to convey movement, 76–77
Aswan, 15, 51, 86
  construction materials from, 68
Ayn Asil, 59–60

Benben stone, 30
Bonaparte, Napoleon, 83
  Commission des Sciences et Arts,
    83
  Description de l'Égypte (Description of
    Egypt), 83
Bureaucratic systems, 3
  advancement of, 6
Byblos, 14

Cairo, 84, 86
  Cairo University, 86
"Canon of proportions," 73
Capstone, 54
Carter, Howard, 84
Causeways, 28–29, 39, 69
Cemetery fields, 62
Censuses, 7, 47

Chambers, 39, 53
  burial, 37
  roofing of, 53
Champollion, Jean-François, 81
Constellations, 21–22
Construction
  directional orientation of, 49
  finishing of, 54
  gnomon used during, 49
  leveling of ground during, 49
  numbers of laborers in, 48
  square level used during, 49
Construction materials
  alabaster, 70
  basalt, 50–51, 68–70
  granite, 50–51, 68–71
  limestone, 50–51, 54, 68, 70
  plaster, 79
  sandstone, 50–51
Coptos, 14
Cosmogony, 22 36
  Heliopolitan, 22
Courtyard in mortuary temples, 27
Cult buildings, 25, 39
Cult of the dead king, 25, 58, 70

Dahshur, 9, 27
  pyramid field of, 5
  pyramid town of, 56
  pyramids at, 53
Dakhleh Oasis, 59–60
Decoration, process of, 79
Decorum, 28
Deir el-Medina, 19
Deities
  Amun, 20–21
  Amun-Re, 20–21; god of the king, 21
  Atum, 22
  Bes, 19

Geb, 22
Hathor, 19; priestesses of, 32, 65
Horus, 5, 19–20, 22; as god of kingship, 19, 21
Isis, 20, 22, 65; as Graeco-Roman deity, 82
Khnum, 69
Khonsu, 20
Min, 18; priestesses of, 32
Neith, priestesses of, 32, 65
Nekhbet, 69
Nephthys, 22, 65
Nun, 22, 36
Nut, 22
Osiris, 5, 22–23, 65; god of the afterlife, 23
Osiris-Serapis, 82
Ptah, priestesses of, 32
Re, 10, 19–20, 24, 30; god of sun's energy and light, 22; in theophoric names, 30
Sekhmet, 19
Seth, 22, 65; animal of, 5
Shu, 22
Tefnut, 22
Thoth, 20
Delta, 3
Destruction of antiquities, 86–87
Divine birth, 19
Droughts, 15
Dynasty Zero, 3
Dynasty Zero, kings of
  Ka, 45
Dynasty One, 3, 5
Dynasty One, kings of
  Aha, 3
  Anedjib, 29, 36
  Den, 3–4, 29, 63
  Narmer, 3
Dynasty Two, 4–6, 8

Dynasty Two, kings of
  Khasekhemwy, 4–6
  Peribsen, 4–6
  Sened, 5
  Weneg, 5
Dynasty Three, 6
Dynasty Three, kings of
  Djoser, 6, 8, 26, 29, 37
Dynasty Four, 5, 9
Dynasty Four, kings of
  Djedefre, 10
  Khafre, 10–11; causeway of, 28
    pyramid town of, 57 valley
    temple of, 40–41, 67
  Khufu, 9–10; priestesses of, 32;
    pyramid complex of, 27; pyramid
    of, 11, 37, 48, 53; pyramid town
    (Akhet-Khufu) of, 57, 62; valley
    temple of, 67
  Menkaure, 11–12, 48, 54; industrial
    activity at pyramid town of, 59;
    pyramid town of, 56, 58; valley
    temple of, 67
  Shepseskaf, 12
  Sneferu, 9–10, 14; pyramid of, 27;
    pyramid towns of, 5; valley
    temple of, 40
Dynasty Five, 5, 13–14, 21
Dynasty Five, kings of
  Djedkare-Isesi, 30
  Menkauhor, 13, 30
  Neferirkare, 31; valley temple of, 67
  Niuserre, pyramid of, 50; pyramid
    complex of, 30; Sahure, 40;
    architecture of valley temple of,
    68–69; art of causeway of, 78;
    valley temple of, 67
  Unas, 13; causeway of, 28, 69;
    Khaemwaset and restoration of
    pyramid, 82; Pyramid Texts in

  pyramid of, 78; valley temple of,
    67
  Userkaf, 13, 27, 30
Dynasty Six, 13–14
Dynasty Six, kings of
  Pepi I, 14, 42
  Pepi II, 15, 40; valley temples of,
    67

Early Dynastic Period, 2–3
Ebla, 14
Egyptomania, 84
Ein el-Gezareen, 59–60
Elephantine, 15, 73
Enclosures, 25–26, 57, 59
Ennead, 21
  Heliopolitan, 23
Entrance hall in mortuary temples,
  27
Eritrea, 7, 14
Ethiopia, 14
Expansionism, 7

Fayuum, construction materials from,
  68
Field of Reeds, 43
First Intermediate Period, 15
Food production, 57
Fortresses, 15
Funerary enclosures, 6

Giza, 5, 11, 27, 48
  construction at, 51
  industrial complex at, 57
  Plateau, 9–10, 12
  pyramid town of, 56–57, 61
  pyramids at, 37, 53
  valley temples at, 67
  Western Cemetery at, 71
  workers' tombs at, 73

Gold, 7
Graffiti, 64

Hauling of stone, 47, 50
Hawara, 46
Heit el Ghourab, 58
Heliopolis, 10
Helwan, 45
Hemaka, 4
Herodotus, 82
Hierakonpolis, 45

Incense, 14
Inner sanctum, 31
Inundations, 7, 12
Iran, 7
Itet, tomb at Meidum of, 74
Ivory labels, 3, 7

Khaemwaset, son of Rameses II, 82
Khafkhufu, 62
King as celestial presence, 75
    as divine being, 17, 23
    in religious affairs, 27
    in sky, 24
Kom el-Hisn, 59–60

Labor pool, 47
Lapis lazuli, 7
Levers, use of, 53
Libya, 14
Literacy, 3
Louvre Museum, 85
Lower Egypt, 2
Luxor, 86
    seat of government at, 14
Luxor Hotel, Las Vegas, 84–85

Magazines, 27
Manetho, 2, 15

Manpower, 47
    corvée organization of, 47, 63
Mason's marks, 48
Mastabas, 11, 36–37, 49
    construction of, 72
    fill of, 71
Meidum, 27–28, 53
    geese from tomb of Itet at, 75
    mastaba at, 49
    pyramid field of, 5, 46
    pyramid town of, 56
Memphis, 4–5, 8, 14, 45
Mining, 6, 10, 14
Mourners, 32
Myths, Osiris, 23

Names of gangs
    Companions of Menkaure, 48
    Drunks of Menkaure, 48–49
Naqada, 2–3
Neferbauptah, 71
Nefertari, tomb of, 87
Negev, Israel, 3
Netjerikhet. *See* Dynasty Three,
    kings of
Nile, 12, 40
    inundation of, 7, 12, 47
    Nile Valley, 4
Ninetjer, 5
Nomes, 8
    nomarchs, 8–9
    nomarchy, 9
Nubia, 7, 14

Obelisk, 30
Obsidian, 7
Offering texts, 38
Ogdoad, 21

Palermo Stone, 2, 10

Pantheon, 17–19, 21
Papyri, administrative (Abusir), 31
Passageways, 53
Pei, I.M., 85
Polytheism, 19
Pottery, 7
Priests, 28
    lector priest (*heri-heb*), 19
    palace attendant (*khenty-shay*, s.;
        khentiu-shay, pl.), 62, 65
Primeval mound, 29, 32, 37
Ptolemies, 82–83
Punt, 14
Pyramid Arena, Memphis, 85
Pyramid complexes, 13, 25, 27, 39
Pyramid fields, 5, 45
    location changes within, 46
    as World Heritage sites, 85
Pyramid Texts, 13, 18–20, 28, 38, 41
    from papyrus copies, 42
    order of, 42
    utterances, 42
Pyramid towns, 56–57, 62
    cemeteries of, 61
    decrees of Pepi I at, 56
    social structures of, 60
Pyramidion, 54
Pyramids, Bent, 9, 40, 52, 56
    Great, 10, 48
    Red, 9, 27, 56

Quarrying, 10, 46–47, 49–50

Ramps, types of, 51–52
    at Sahure's valley temple, 68
Rebellion, Dynasty Two, 5
Reliefwork, 25, 35, 38
    in causeways, 28
    direction of figures in, 75
    in nonroyal tombs, 18, 24

painted, 77, 79
    programs of, 74, 77
    registers in, 76
    sporting tableaux in, 77
    subjects of, 74
    subjects of in nonroyal tombs,
        79–80
    in valley temples, 68–69
Religious ideology, 18, 29
Religious symbolism, 29
Ritual, 24, 28, 31, 40, 76
    diurnal, 31
    noctural, 31
Rosetta Stone, 83
    languages of, 83
Royal landholdings, 7, 9, 11

Sacred space, 26, 39
Saqqara, 5–6, 36
    Early Dynastic tombs at, 45
    North, 29
    pyramid town of, 56
    royal necropolis of, 13
    South, 11, 30
    Step Pyramid at, 37
    valley temples at South Saqqara, 67
Seals, 3, 7
Sed Festival, 8, 27, 32
Seila, 9
Serdab, 25, 41, 72
Seti I, 87
Shrines, 19
Silver, 7
Sinai, 6–7, 14
Statue niches in mortuary temples, 27
Step Pyramid, 6, 29, 37
Sun
    cult of, 10, 31
    worship of, 22, 30
Supreme Council of Antiquities, 87

Syncretism, 20
Syria-Palestine, 4, 7, 14–15

Taxation, 7
Tell el-Amarna, 19
Temples, 17, 19, 24, 39
  architectural and symbolic
    development of, 39
  architectural symbolism of, 40
  components of mortuary, 70
  endowments, 12
  hierarchy, 31
  mortuary, 25–27, 38, 48, 69–71
  sun, 30
  valley, 25, 27, 30, 40, 58, 67
  valley, use of, 41
Thebes. *See* Luxor
Timber, 14
Titles
  nsw-bity, 4
  other, 62
  royal, 10
  Son of Re, 10
  women's religious, 65
Tjetu, 62
Tombs, 5, 71
Trade, 7, 10
  routes, 14
Triad, 21

Turin Canon, 2, 6, 12
Turquoise, 7
Tutankhamun, 84

Umm el-Qaab, 3, 39, 45
Unification, 2
Upper Egypt, 2

Valley of the Kings, 86
Vizier, 8

Wall of the Crow, 58
  reasons for, 58
Winding Waterway, 43
Women
  overseers of doctors, 65
  overseers of palace attendants,
    65
  roles of, 64
Work crews
  daily, 48
  divisions of, 63
  earliest evidence for phyles of, 63
  gangs of, 48–40, 63
  phyle names of, 63
  phyles of, 31, 48–49, 63
World Heritage, 85

Zagazig University, 86

About the Author

JENNIFER HELLUM is a lecturer at the University of Auckland, New Zealand. She has taught at universities in North America, and has excavated in Egypt on the Red Sea coast, the Delta, the Giza plateau, and in Middle Egypt.